PROBABILITY AND STATISTICAL INFERENCE
FOR ENGINEERS

UNIVERSITY TEXTS IN THE MATHEMATICAL SCIENCES

HERBERT E. ROBBINS, *Editor*

PROBABILITY and
STATISTICAL INFERENCE
for Engineers

A FIRST COURSE

CYRUS DERMAN and MORTON KLEIN
COLUMBIA UNIVERSITY

NEW YORK

OXFORD UNIVERSITY PRESS

1959

PRINTED IN THE UNITED STATES OF AMERICA

Preface

THE PURPOSE of this book is to present, in a compact form, a one-semester course of study in probability theory and statistical inference. It is directed toward engineering students who have had the usual undergraduate courses in integral and differential calculus.

The treatment of the subject matter is in accord with modern developments in probability theory and statistical inference. It is intended that this material will provide the student with enough fundamentals for competent professional application, and with a sufficient degree of mathematical maturity to enable further study, particularly in other courses consistent with a modern, analytically oriented engineering curriculum.

The volume has its origins in a set of notes prepared for an undergraduate course offered in the Department of Industrial and Management Engineering at the School of Engineering, Columbia University. We are indebted to Professor Herbert Robbins for encouraging us to prepare this text from the notes. We also appreciate his careful reading of the manuscript and his clarifying suggestions.

Acknowledgements are also due to Professor A. Sledge for helpful remarks; to Mr. Arthur Veinott, Jr., for many problem suggestions; to Mrs. Ruth Edelstein and Mrs. Janet Wehner for patient and skillful secretarial efforts.

We are indebted to Professor Sir Ronald A. Fisher, Cambridge, to Dr. Frank Yates, Rothamsted, and to

Messrs. Oliver and Boyd Ltd., Edinburgh, for permission to abridge Table No. III from their book *Statistical Tables for Biological, Agricultural, and Medical Research*.

C. D.
M. K.

Columbia University
New York, N.Y.
February, 1959

CONTENTS

REFERENCES

THE reader will find useful supplementary material among the books listed below. Under *Suggested Reading* pertinent sections of the books in this list have been correlated with the sections of the text to which they apply.

ALLENDOERFER, C. B., and OAKLEY, C. O., *Principles of Mathematics* (New York: McGraw-Hill, 1955).

MAY, K. O., *Fundamental Mathematics* (Cambridge: Addison-Wesley, 1955).

KEMENY, J. G., SNELL, J. L., and THOMPSON, G. L., *Introduction to Finite Mathematics* (Englewood Cliffs: Prentice-Hall, 1957).

FELLER, W., *An Introduction to Probability Theory and its Applications* (New York: J. Wiley & Sons, Second Edition, 1957).

CRAMÉR, H., *The Elements of Probability Theory* (New York: J. Wiley & Sons, 1955).

HOEL, P. G., *Introduction to Mathematical Statistics* (New York: J. Wiley & Sons, Second Edition, 1954).

MOOD, A. F., *Introduction to the Theory of Statistics* (New York: McGraw-Hill, 1950).

BOWKER, A. H., and LIEBERMAN, G. J., (a) *Handbook of Industrial Statistics* (Englewood Cliffs: Prentice-Hall, 1955).

—— (b) *Engineering Statistics* (Englewood Cliffs: Prentice-Hall, 1959).

LUCE, R. D., and RAIFFA, H., *Games and Decisions* (New York: J. Wiley & Sons, 1957).

SUGGESTED READING

After page 8

    1. Allendoerfer and Oakley, Chapters 5 and 6.

    2. May, Chapters 3 and 5.

    3. Kemeny, Snell, and Thompson, pp. 54–78.

After page 13

    Feller, pp. 1–18.

After page 27

   1. Feller, pp. 19–24.
   2. Cramér, pp. 11–34, 57–65.
   3. Hoel, pp. 1–8, 15–24.

After page 37

   1. Feller, pp. 149–54, 164–8.
   2. Mood, pp. 192–6.
   3. Hoel, pp. 211–14.

After page 50

   1. Mood, pp. 93–100.
   2. Cramér, pp. 71, 74–8, 81–2.

After page 64

   1. Cramér, pp. 65–70, 72–4.
   2. Mood, pp. 74–83.
   3. Feller, pp. 215–19, 221–2.

After page 72

   1. Feller, pp. 104–21.
   2. Cramér, pp. 35–8.
   3. Kemeny, Snell, and Thompson, pp. 129–38.

After page 80

   1. Feller, pp. 135–9, 141–2.
   2. Cramér, pp. 69–70.

After page 91

   1. Feller, pp. 142–9, 168–78.
   2. Cramér, pp. 96–104, 113–15.
   3. Hoel, pp. 67–70, 82–8.

After page 100

   1. Hoel, pp. 196–202.
   2. Bowker and Lieberman (*b*), Chapter 8.

After page 120

Luce and Raiffa, Chapter 13.

After page 139

   1. Cramér, pp. 190–213.
   2. Hoel, pp. 20–38, 88–94, 103–13, 203–8, 219–29.
   3. Bowker and Lieberman (*a*), pp. 800–8, 848–73.
   4. Bowker and Lieberman (*b*), Chapter 6.

Introduction

ONE OF THE DIFFICULTIES encountered by the engineer in the course of his problem-solving activities is that caused by variation. This occurs mainly because of limitations on the control of experimental and industrial procedures, measurement errors, and the inconstant nature of the phenomena under study. For example, in data representing the output of an engineering process, the presence of variation makes the problem of describing that process and comparing it with others non-trivial.

Suppose an engineer has performed tests on two processes which have yielded the following numerical results:

Process A: 32, 25, 12, 25, 16, 20, 19, 26, 24

Process B: 10, 27, 18, 25, 13, 16, 12, 14, 20.

How can he use these numbers to characterize these processes? How can he predict the future behavior of these processes? If a choice between the two processes is required, how should he make this choice?

In considering questions of this kind it has been observed that many engineering processes yield data that appear as if they were generated by some chance mechanism; for example, by rolling a pair of dice. Thus, from our experience with games of chance, if the process were to be observed many times we would expect to see numbers repeating, and, eventually, to see the relative frequency of their occurrences settle down, at least approximately, to some fixed quantity. This property, possessed by many processes, is sometimes called *statistical regularity*. Questions such as those raised in the above example can be treated rationally when dealing with phenomena exhibiting statistical regularity.

Formal descriptions of physical phenomena are usually couched in the language of mathematics. The branch of mathematics which has been developed for the description of phenomena exhibiting statistical regularity is the *theory of probability* (originally conceived for the purpose of solving problems arising in gambling games). Based on the theory of probability, *statistical inference* is that discipline which supplies a methodology for description, prediction, and rational decision making despite the complications which arise due to variation. In what follows we shall present some of the basic ideas of these two important subjects.

1

PRELIMINARIES

1.1. *Elements of set theory*

Definition 1.1: A *set* is a collection of objects.

These objects are usually called either *elements* or *points*. From the viewpoint of mathematics, they are basic building blocks and neither require nor are capable of further definition. However, if they are utilized in a mathematical model which is interpretable in engineering terms, they will denote specific objects or will be otherwise identifiable.

Example 1.1: The set which consists of all defective bolts manufactured in a factory during a particular day. In this case the bolts are the elements. This set contains a finite number of elements.

Example 1.2: The set of all real numbers within the interval extending from zero to one. This contains an infinite number of elements.

As a method of abbreviating the verbal descriptions of sets, especially small sets, it is convenient to include the elements of the set within a pair of braces. For example, the set consisting of the letters a, b, and c would be abbreviated as $\{a, b, c\}$.

Definition 1.2: The totality of all elements under consideration is usually referred to as a *space*. Hence, a space consists of elements, any collection of which is a set.

Example 1.3: In the previous examples there could be, respectively, the space consisting of all bolts (defective and otherwise) produced by the factory during a day; and the space consisting of all the real numbers. Whenever a set is discussed, it is always considered (although usually not specified) with reference to some space.

Operations, defined below (as addition, multiplication, and subtraction are operations on numbers), may be performed on sets.

Definition 1.3: The *union* of two sets, A and B, denoted by $A \cup B$, is the set consisting of all elements which belong *either* to set A *or* to set B.

Example 1.4: Let A denote the set of all bolts manufactured on Monday and Tuesday of a particular week and let B denote the set of all bolts manufactured on Tuesday and Wednesday of the same week. Then, $A \cup B$ denotes the set of all bolts manufactured on Monday, Tuesday, and Wednesday.

Definition 1.4: The *intersection* of two sets, A and B, denoted by $A \cap B$, is the set consisting of all elements which belong to *both A and B.*

Example 1.5: In the previous example, $A \cap B$ denotes the set of bolts which are manufactured on Tuesday.

The definitions of the union and intersection operations are readily extended to groups of more than two sets.

Definition 1.5: The *complement* of a set A, denoted by A^*, is the set of all elements in the space which are not members of A.

Example 1.6: If a space consists of all bolts manufactured during a particular week and if the set A denotes all bolts produced on Monday and Tuesday, then A^* is the set of all bolts produced during the remainder of the week.

Definition 1.6: If C and D are two sets which have no common elements, then $C \cap D$ is a set which contains no elements. This is called the *empty set* and is denoted by ϕ. C and D are then said to be *disjoint*.

The complement of the empty set is the space.

Definition 1.7: The *absolute value* of a number a, denoted by $|a|$, is its numerical value neglecting its algebraic sign; e.g. $|-5| = 5$, $|5| = 5$.

Example 1.7: The following are sets of real numbers, each with generic element denoted by x.

(1) $\{|x| \leqslant a\} = \{-a \leqslant x \leqslant 0\} \cup \{0 \leqslant x \leqslant a\}$
$$= \{-a \leqslant x \leqslant a\}.$$

(2) $\{|x| > a\} = \{x > a\} \cup \{x < -a\}.$

(3) $\{|x-b| \leqslant a\} = \{-a \leqslant x-b \leqslant 0\} \cup \{0 \leqslant x-b \leqslant a\}$
$$= \{b-a \leqslant x \leqslant b\} \cup \{b \leqslant x \leqslant b+a\}$$
$$= \{b-a \leqslant x \leqslant b+a\}.$$

(4) $\{|x-b| > a\} = \{x-b > a\} \cup \{x-b < -a\}$
$$= \{x > a+b\} \cup \{x < b-a\}.$$

NOTE: (1) is read as the set of all real numbers, x, whose absolute value is less than or equal to a.

1.2. *Functions*

Suppose there exist two sets denoted by X and Y. Then, a particular kind of relationship between the elements of each set may exist such that a new set can be formed whose elements consist of ordered pairs of elements, each pair consisting of one element from each of the original sets. Thus, if $X = \{x_1, x_2, x_3\}$ and $Y = \{y_1, y_2, y_3\}$, then one new set of ordered pairs could be $\{(x_2, y_2), (x_1, y_1), (x_3, y_3)\}$.† For example, X might denote a set of bolts and Y the set of numbers representing the length of each of the bolts. Then it is natural to pair a bolt with its length. This new set of pairs is an illustration of what is meant by a function. However, a qualification is required. In the above example, it is conceivable that two or more of the bolts may have the same length. Thus, if $y_1 = y_2$ the set of pairs could be designated by $\{(x_1, y_1), (x_2, y_1), (x_3, y_3)\}$. It is not conceivable, however, that one bolt could have two different lengths. Thus, a set of the form $\{(x_1, y_1), (x_1, y_2)\}$ is not permitted if $y_1 \neq y_2$.

This concept may be formalized as follows:

Definition 1.8: A *function* is a set of ordered pairs of elements such that for each first member of a pair there exists a *unique* second member.

Example 1.8: The Morse code is a function, in the form of a catalogue of relationships between the letters of the alphabet and combinations of dots and dashes such that each letter is represented by a unique combination of symbols.

It is usually unnecessary to define a function by listing in full detail the set of all ordered pairs. For example, if a set of ordered pairs is $\{(1, 1), (2, 4), ..., (100, 10,000)\}$ then the implied rule of association between the first 100 natural numbers and their squares can be taken advantage of to describe the function in a concise manner. Another tech-

† Note that the ordering has reference to the order of writing the *members of a pair* and not the order of writing the pairs.

nique of definition could then be to describe the first of the original sets together with the implied rule of association which enables the description of the second set. For the above case, if

$$X = \{1, 2,..., 100\} \quad \text{and} \quad Y = \{1, 4,..., 10{,}000\},$$

the function could be written as

$$\{y = x^2, \text{ where } x = 1, 2,..., 100\}$$

where x and y denote the generic elements of X and Y.

Definition 1.9: The set of elements which are listed as the first members in each of the ordered pairs of a function is called the *domain of definition* of the function. Similarly, the set of elements listed second is called the *range* of the function. The phrase 'values of a function' is commonly used to denote the values or labels assigned to the elements of the range.

The specification of the domain of definition together with a rule of association is sufficient to define a function, since the set of ordered pairs can always be derived from this information.

Consequently, the following definition is equivalent to the definition given earlier:

Definition 1.10: A *function* is a rule, a domain of definition, and a range such that for each element in the domain there is associated, by the rule, one and only one element in the range.

The notation and form given below will be used. Let f designate a function which consists of ordered pairs $\{x, f(x)\}$ where x is an arbitrary element in the domain of definition and $f(x)$ is the unique element in the range associated with x. Then, for the example considered earlier, the complete description would be written

$$f: \quad f(x) = x^2 \quad \text{where } x = 1, 2,\ldots, 100.$$

This is to be read as: The function f such that corresponding to each element x in the domain, there is associated, by the rule $f(x) = x^2$, an element $f(x)$ in the range; the domain consists of the set of positive integers from 1 to 100. It is important to emphasize, as in Example 1.8 and as in functions g and A in Example 1.9, that neither the domain nor the range of a function need be numbers.

Example 1.9: Some typical functions are listed in the table below.

The function	Element of the range	The rule	The domain
S	$S(b)$	$S(b) = 7$	$-\infty < b < \infty$
h	$h(z)$	$h(z) = 3z$ if $-\infty < z \leqslant 0$ $= 5$ if $0 < z \leqslant 10$ $= 6z^2$ if $12 \leqslant z$	
g	$g(B)$	$g(B) = \text{Good}$ if $2 \leqslant B \leqslant 3$ $= \text{Defective}$ otherwise	
A	$A(x, y, r)$	$A(x, y, r) = \pi r^2$	All circles with center (x, y) where $\begin{pmatrix} -\infty < x < \infty \\ -\infty < y < \infty \end{pmatrix}$ and radius r $(r \geqslant 0)$
m	$m(x)$	$\min(x, x^2)$, i.e. $$m(x) = \begin{cases} x^2 & \text{if } 0 < x \leqslant 1 \\ x & \text{if } 1 \leqslant x < 2 \end{cases}$$	$0 < x < 2$
a	a_i†	$a_i = i^2$	$i = 1,\ldots, 100$

† The element in the domain of definition is sometimes indicated by a subscript.

Example 1.10: It will be recalled from elementary calculus that if the quantity called the definite integral of a function f exists, it can be computed according to the rule

$$F(b)-F(a) = \int_a^b f(t)\,dt \qquad (a < b)$$

where F denotes any function such that

$$F'(t) = f(t)$$

and where the upper and lower limits of integration, b and a respectively, are elements in the domain of f.

If the upper limit of integration is taken to be an arbitrary element, x, in the domain of f, then the integral of f can be defined as a function of its upper limit. This function, here denoted by I, is written in the form

$$I: \quad I(x) = \int_a^x f(t)\,dt = F(x)-F(a).$$

Suppose $f(t) = t$, $a = 1$. Then

$$I: \quad I(x) = \int_1^x t\,dt = \tfrac{1}{2}x^2 - \tfrac{1}{2}.$$

1.3. *Notation*

Listed below are notational forms which will be utilized throughout.

1.3.1. THE SIGMA NOTATION

Definition 1.11:

$$\sum_{i=1}^n a_i = a_1 + a_2 + \ldots + a_n.$$

The numbers 1 and n are called the limits of summation (analogous to the limits of integration). Sometimes the domain of summation will be indicated beneath the summation sign; e.g. $\sum_{i \geqslant k} a_i$ indicates that the summand (a_i) is to be summed for all values of i which are greater than or equal to the number k.

The following properties follow easily from the definition:

(1) $\sum_{i=1}^{n} a_i = \sum_{i=1}^{k} a_i + \sum_{i=k+1}^{n} a_i.$

(2) $\sum_{i=1}^{n} ca_i = c \sum_{i=1}^{n} a_i$ where c is a constant.

(3) $\sum_{i=1}^{n} c = nc.$

(4) $\sum_{i=1}^{n} (a_i + b_i) = \sum_{i=1}^{n} a_i + \sum_{i=1}^{n} b_i.$

(5) $\left(\sum_{i=1}^{n} a_i \right)^2 = \sum_{i=1}^{n} (a_i^2) + 2 \sum_{i=1}^{n-1} \sum_{k=i+1}^{n} a_i a_k.$

1.3.2. THE PRODUCT NOTATION
Definition 1.12:
$$\prod_{i=1}^{n} a_i = (a_1)(a_2)...(a_n).$$

A special case of interest is

$$\prod_{i=1}^{n} (i) = n(n-1)(n-2)...(1) = n!$$

EXERCISES—I

NOTE: In all exercises, when the student is asked to *describe* a function, it is meant that he should describe the domain of definition and the rule which assigns points in the range. In cases in which the domain consists of a small number of points, an actual listing of all the pairs is requested.

1. A, B, and C are sets in a space which consists of twenty-six elements each identified by a lower-case letter of the alphabet.

Suppose that
$$A = \{a, b, c, d, e\}$$
$$B = \{b, d, f, h, j\}$$
$$C = \{c, f, i, l, o\}.$$

Find:

(a) $A \cup B$, $B \cup C$, $A \cup B \cup C$.

(b) $A \cap B$, $B \cap C$, $A \cap B \cap C$.

(c) $(A \cup B \cup C)^*$, $(A \cap B \cap C)^*$.

(d) $(A \cup B) \cap (A \cup B^*)$.

(e) $(A \cup B) \cap (A^* \cup B) \cap (A \cup B^*)$.

2. Find the sets of real numbers, with generic elements denoted by x, which satisfy the following conditions:

(a) $|x-5| = 2$.

(b) $|x-5| < 2$.

(c) $|x-5| \geqslant 2$.

(d) $|x+5| = 2$.

(e) $|x+5| \leqslant 2$.

(f) $|x+5| > 2$.

3. A function R is given by the following table, where n denotes an element in its domain of definition:

$R(n)$	n
$0 \cdot 5n$	0–50
$0 \cdot 3n$	51–75
$0 \cdot 2n$	76–100

(a) Draw the graph of this function.

(b) If the domain is restricted to integer values between (and including) the numbers 73 to 77, describe the function R as a set of ordered pairs.

4. The marginal revenue (f) in dollars per gallon from the sale of a certain chemical can be defined by the function:

$$f: \quad f(G) = \begin{cases} 1, & \text{for } 0 \leqslant G < 2 \\ 2, & \text{for } 2 \leqslant G < 3 \\ 4, & \text{for } 3 \leqslant G < 5 \\ 5, & \text{for } 5 \leqslant G \end{cases}$$

where G = number of gallons of the chemical sold.

    (*a*) Write the definite integral whose range specifies the total revenue from the sale of any non-negative quantity of the chemical.

    (*b*) What is the total revenue from the sale of 5 gallons?

5. Let $z_1 = 5$; $z_2 = -3$; $z_3 = 1$; $z_4 = 8$.

    $y_1 = 7$; $y_2 = 2$; $y_3 = -1$; $y_4 = 1$.

Find:

    (*a*) $\left(\sum\limits_{i=1}^{4} z_i \right)\left(\sum\limits_{i=1}^{4} y_i \right).$

    (*b*) $\left(\sum\limits_{i=1}^{4} z_i^2 \right).$

    (*c*) $\left(\sum\limits_{i=1}^{4} z_i \right)^2.$

    (*d*) $\sum\limits_{i=1}^{4} z_i y_i.$

    (*e*) $\prod\limits_{i=1}^{4} y_i.$

    (*f*) $\prod\limits_{i=1}^{4} y_i z_i.$

6. Describe the function given below by performing the required integration.

$$G: \quad G(t) = \int_0^t \min(1, x)\, dx \quad \text{where} \quad 0 \leqslant t \leqslant 2.$$

    (Hint: First sketch the graph of the integrand.)

7. A function f is given by

$$f: \quad f(x) = \begin{cases} x & \text{if} \quad 0 \leqslant x \leqslant 1 \\ x^2 & \text{if} \quad 1 < x \leqslant 2 \\ x^3 & \text{if} \quad 2 < x \leqslant 3 \end{cases}.$$

Describe

$$G: \quad G(t) = \int_0^t f(x)\, dx \quad \text{where} \quad 0 \leqslant t \leqslant 3.$$

2

ELEMENTS OF PROBABILITY THEORY

2.1. *The sample space*

Definition 2.1: An *experiment* is any well-defined action.

Example 2.1: Toss a coin once in some prescribed manner.

Example 2.2: Toss a coin five times in some prescribed manner.

Example 2.3: Draw an item from a group of six as follows: Assign numbers 1, 2,..., 6 to the items so that no two have the same number. Roll a die. Select the item whose assigned number corresponds to that shown on the die.

Definition 2.2: Each possible result of an experiment, which is of interest, is called an *outcome*.

Example 2.4: In Example 2.1 there are two outcomes: {Heads, Tails}.

Example 2.5: In Example 2.2 there are 2^5 possible results: e.g. (H, T, T, H, H) meaning heads on the first toss, tails on the second,..., etc.—is a typical outcome.

Definition 2.3: The totality of outcomes is called the *sample space* (denoted by Ω). An outcome is sometimes referred to as a point in the sample space.

Definition 2.4 : An *event* is a set of outcomes.

An event is said to have occurred if an experiment results in any outcome which is an element of the event.

It should be noted that there are many possible events associated with experiments. For convenience, the set consisting of no outcomes also is considered to be an event. It is called the *null event* (denoted by ϕ). The sample space also is considered to be an event. For example, with an experiment which can result in three possible outcomes, denoted a, b, and c, we may associate the following events:

(1)	$\{\phi\}$.	(5)	$\{a,b\}$.
(2)	$\{a\}$.	(6)	$\{a,c\}$.
(3)	$\{b\}$.	(7)	$\{b,c\}$.
(4)	$\{c\}$.	(8)	$\{a,b,c\} = \Omega$.

Example 2.6: An experiment consists of tossing a coin twice. One event is that of heads occurring on the first toss. This event consists of two points. In brace notation, it may be written as $\{(H, T), (H, H)\}$.

Another event is the set of outcomes in which either heads occurs on the first toss or tails on the second toss. This may be denoted as $\{(H, H), (H, T), (T, T)\}$.

From given events, new events can be derived by performing the operations of union, intersection, and complementation; e.g. the union of $\{(H, T), (H, H), (T, H)\}$ with $\{(H, T), (H, H), (T, T)\}$ is the event

$$\{(H, T), (H, H), (T, H), (T, T)\};$$

the intersection of the above two events is $\{(H, T), (H, H)\}$; and the complement of the first event is $\{(T, T)\}$. The intersection of $\{(H,H),(H,T)\}$ with $\{(T,H)\}$ is the null event ϕ.

Example 2.7: An experiment consists of exploring a tract of land. The outcomes are of too complex a nature to describe easily; however, some events of interest are: (1) finding oil, (2) finding gas, (3) finding nothing, and (4) finding both gas and oil.

Let E_1 denote the event of finding oil,

E_2 denote the event of finding gas.

Then, $E_3 = E_1 \cup E_2$ is the event in which either oil or gas is found,

$E_4 = E_1 \cap E_2$ denotes the event in which both oil and gas are found, and

$E_5 = E_3^*$ is the event in which neither oil nor gas is found.

EXERCISES—II

An experiment consists of drawing three flash bulbs from a lot and classifying them as defective or non-defective.

If a bulb is defective, assign the letter D to it.

If a bulb is good, assign the letter G to it.

A drawing could then be described, for example, by the triplet (D, G, G) indicating that the first bulb was defective and the remaining two were good.

Let E_1 denote the event—the first bulb drawn was defective.

Let E_2 denote the event—the second bulb drawn was defective.

Let E_3 denote the event—the third bulb drawn was defective.

Describe the sample space and list all outcomes in:

(a) E_1.	(e) $E_1 \cup E_3$.	(h) $E_1 \cap E_2$.
(b) E_2.	(f) $E_2 \cup E_3$.	(i) $E_1 \cap E_3$.
(c) E_3.	(g) $E_1 \cup E_2 \cup E_3$.	(j) $E_2 \cap E_3$.
(d) $E_1 \cup E_2$.		(k) $E_1 \cap E_2 \cap E_3$.

2.2. *Random variables*

Definition 2.5: A *random variable* is a numerically valued function defined over the sample space; i.e. it is a rule which assigns a number to each outcome of an experiment.

The notion of a random variable arises naturally within the context of an experiment. Outcomes of an experiment in themselves may be extremely complex and may even defy complete description. The role of a random variable, for these conditions, is to permit a description of the outcome which retains its essential features. Usually it will represent some measurement of interest to the experimenter. With any particular experiment it is possible to define many random variables. The experimenter works with those of interest to him (usually those which reflect the properties of the outcomes which are considered important).

Random variables of engineering interest may be classified as follows:

(1) *Discrete* random variables are those which take on a finite or denumerable† number of values.

Example 2.8: An experiment consists of tossing a coin R times.

(*a*) One possible random variable is the rule which assigns to the outcome a value corresponding to the number of heads in the outcome.

(*b*) Another possible random variable is the rule which assigns to an outcome a value corresponding to the number of tosses before the first head is obtained; e.g. associated with the outcome $(T, T, H, ..., T)$ is the number 2.

† A set is called denumerable if its elements can be put into a one-to-one correspondence with the set of positive integers 1, 2, 3,... .

   (2) *Continuous* random variables are those which take
   on a continuum of values.

Example 2.9: An experiment consists of distilling some
alcohol. The quantity of alcohol produced is best regarded
as a continuous random variable. (NOTE: The *measured*
quantity produced is actually a discrete random variable
because of the limitations of measuring instruments.)

Example 2.10: Consider the experiment of firing a projectile at a target. Assume the existence of a coordinate
system superimposed on the target with the origin placed
at the center.

   (*a*) One random variable could be the rule assigning the
value of the abscissa corresponding to the point of impact
of the projectile.

   (*b*) Another possible random variable is the rule assigning the ordinate value of the projectile position.

   (*c*) A third could be the rule yielding the distance of the
projectile from the origin.

   Random variables will be denoted by capital letters such
as X, Y, and Z. An outcome will be denoted by the letter
ω. Thus, $X(\omega)$ denotes the value of the random variable
X associated with the outcome ω.

   In Example 2.10, X could stand for the abscissa value,
Y for the ordinate, and $Z = \sqrt{(X^2 + Y^2)}$ for the distance
Note that X^2, Y^2, and Z^2 are also random variables; i.e.
for a given outcome ω there are corresponding values of
X^2, Y^2, and Z^2.

Example 2.11: An experiment consists of observing the
things which occur in the emergency ward of a hospital on
a particular day.

The sample space for this experiment is clearly a complex affair which defies complete description. However, the experimenter's interests, expressed in terms of random variables, enable one to by-pass the description of the sample space and to concentrate directly on the pertinent aspects of the experiment's outcomes.

As an example, the random variable N could denote the number of patients arriving who require certain X-ray examinations. N could take on integer values ranging from zero to the maximum number of people (not necessarily known) who could possibly arrive at the particular emergency ward being observed.

As another example, suppose that the ward is such that it can only handle 100 such patients per day at cost (to the hospital) equal to $7.00 per patient. Further, if more than 100 such patients arrive the hospital is required to ship this excess to another hospital at cost (to the hospital) equal to $10.00 per patient.

If the total cost to the hospital, C, is a random variable of interest, it may be defined as follows:

$$C: \quad C(N) = \begin{cases} \$7.00N & \text{if } 0 \leqslant N \leqslant 100 \\ \$700.00 + \$10.00(N-100) & \text{if } 100 < N \end{cases}$$

where $N = 0, 1, 2, \ldots$.

EXERCISES—III

1. With reference to the flash bulb experiment described in Exercise II, describe five different random variables which are of some possible interest.

2. Suppose that a plant consists of two separate production lines, each of which feeds the same product into a stockpile. The productive capacity of one line is five units per day and that of the other is three units per day. An experiment consists of observing

the behavior of the stockpile at the end of a day in which both lines were operating. If it is assumed that the output of each line is a random variable which can take on integer values from zero up to capacity,

  (a) Describe the random variable denoting the condition of the stockpile after one day's production.
  (b) Repeat (a) for the condition of the stockpile after two days' production.

3. A production line consists of two work stations in a series arrangement. Let X be a random variable denoting the production rate in units per day of one station and Y a random variable describing the production rate at the other station. The resulting production rate of the line is controlled by the lower of the two in any particular day. Assume that the experiment is to run the line for one day, and let G_1 be a random variable describing the output of the line, i.e. $G_1(X, Y) = \min(X, Y)$. (Assume that both the ranges of X and Y are the integers from zero to three.)

  (a) Describe G_1 completely.

Let G_2 be the random variable describing the behavior of the inventory (assuming no withdrawals) after two days' production.

  (b) Describe G_2 completely.

4. A production situation consists of one machine (A) feeding material into a bank at the end of one hour's production and another machine (B) withdrawing material from the bank at the start of the next hour's production. Let X be a random variable describing the output of machine A, and Y a random variable describing the withdrawals for machine B. Assume that the range of X is $\{0, 1, 2, 3\}$ and that of Y is $\{0, 1, 2\}$.

  (a) Describe the random variable G_1 which denotes the condition of the stockpile after one hour's production.
  (b) Describe G_2 (the random variable denoting the stockpile condition after two hours' production).

5. The number of oil tankers (N) arriving at a certain refinery on any day is a random variable. Present port facilities can service three tankers a day. If more than three tankers arrive in a day, the tankers in excess of three must be sent to another port at a cost of $2,000 per tanker sent away.

(a) Describe the random variable representing the number of tankers serviced on any day.

(b) Describe the random variable representing the number of tankers turned away on any day.

(c) Describe the random variable which denotes the refinery's loss on any day.

6. A small bakery has found that the demand (V) for fresh bread on any day is a random variable whose range is $\{0 \leqslant V \leqslant 100 \text{ lb.}\}$. The profit per pound of fresh bread sold is \$0.10. If bread is not sold on the day it is baked, it can be sold in unlimited quantities on the next day at a loss of \$0.05/lb. Assume that the demand for fresh bread is not affected by the amount of day-old bread sold. Let b denote the actual amount of bread baked on a day.

(a) Describe the random variable which represents the unsatisfied daily demand, i.e. lost sales.

(b) Describe the random variable which represents the amount of bread sold.

(c) Describe the random variable which represents the daily profit to the baker.

2.3. *Probability*

Definition 2.6: With a given experiment, we assume the existence of a function, P, which assigns a number, $P\{E\}$, to each event E in the sample space. This number is called the *probability* of event E.

Some properties of this function are:

(1) $P\{\Omega\} = 1$.

(2) $P\{\phi\} = 0$.

(3) $0 \leqslant P\{E\} \leqslant 1$.

(4) $P\{E_1 \cup E_2\} = P\{E_1\} + P\{E_2\} - P\{E_1 \cap E_2\}$.

NOTE: If $E_1 \cap E_2 = \phi$ (these are said to be mutually exclusive or disjoint events), then

$$P\{E_1 \cup E_2\} = P\{E_1\} + P\{E_2\}.$$

The *frequency interpretation* of probability is of special interest to engineers.

Let n = the number of times an experiment is repeated,

$n\{E\}$ = the number of times which some event E has occurred during the n trials.

We *assume*
$$\lim_{n \to \infty} \frac{n\{E\}}{n} = P\{E\}.$$

It is assumed that the relative frequency of the event E approaches the probability of the event E as the number of trials of the experiment increases. This assumption is the connection between the purely *mathematical* idea of a probability and the *empirical* evidence of regularities in the behavior of certain events in sequences of repeated experiments. Such correspondences between relative frequencies and assigned probabilities are well known to exist in most gambling games. Statistical regularities have also been found to exist in physical phenomena of interest to engineers such as vacuum-tube life expectancy, occurrences of defectives in manufactured products, errors in clerical operations, machine breakdowns, etc. When evidence of such regularities is lacking, one should be hesitant about applying probability theory.

The postulated properties (1), (2), (3), and (4) of a probability function reflect the behavior of the relative frequency $n\{E\}/n$. To see this, it is easily verified that for any n

(1') $n\{\Omega\} = n$.

(2') $n\{\phi\} = 0$.

(3') $0 \leqslant n\{E\} \leqslant n$.

(4') $n\{E_1 \cup E_2\} = n\{E_1\} + n\{E_2\} - n\{E_1 \cap E_2\}$.

On dividing through by n, we see that (1′), (2′), (3′), and (4′) are the properties (1), (2), (3), and (4) with $n\{E\}/n$ substituted for $P\{E\}$.

Example 2.12: An experiment consists of taking two photographs and printing and rating them as either satisfactorily exposed, underexposed, or overexposed. Let these three conditions be denoted respectively by s, u, and o. Then the sample space is

$$\Omega = \begin{cases} (s,s) & (s,u) & (s,o) \\ (u,s) & (u,u) & (u,o) \\ (o,s) & (o,u) & (o,o) \end{cases}.$$

Suppose it is known that the probabilities associated with each of the outcomes in Ω are as listed below:

$$P\{s,s\} = P\{u,u\} = P\{o,o\} = 0\cdot12,$$
$$P\{u,s\} = P\{s,u\} = 0\cdot20,$$
$$P\{s,o\} = P\{o,s\} = P\{o,u\} = P\{u,o\} = 0\cdot06.$$

Some events which might be of interest are:

$E_1 =$ one or more satisfactory prints are obtained.

$E_2 =$ two satisfactory prints are obtained.

$E_3 =$ exactly one overexposed print is obtained.

Then,

$$P\{E_1\} = P\{(s,s) \quad (s,u) \quad (s,o) \quad (u,s) \quad (o,s)\}$$
$$= 0\cdot12 + 0\cdot20 + 0\cdot06 + 0\cdot20 + 0\cdot06 = 0\cdot64,$$
$$P\{E_2\} = P\{(s,s)\} = 0\cdot12,$$
$$P\{E_3\} = P\{(s,o) \quad (o,s) \quad (u,o) \quad (o,u)\}$$
$$= 0\cdot06 + 0\cdot06 + 0\cdot06 + 0\cdot06 = 0\cdot24.$$

Further,

$$P\{E_1 \cap E_2\} = P\{(s, s)\} = 0 \cdot 12,$$
$$P\{E_1 \cup E_2\} = P\{E_1\} + P\{E_2\} - P\{E_1 \cap E_2\}$$
$$= 0 \cdot 64 + 0 \cdot 12 - 0 \cdot 12 = 0 \cdot 64,$$
$$P\{E_2 \cap E_3\} = P\{\phi\} = 0,$$
$$P\{E_2 \cup E_3\} = 0 \cdot 12 + 0 \cdot 24 = 0 \cdot 36,$$
$$P\{E_1 \cap E_3\} = P\{(o, s), \quad (s, o)\} = 0 \cdot 12.$$

2.4. *Distribution functions*

For any random variable $X = X(\omega)$ of interest, a basic task is to ascribe probabilities to events of the form

$$E_a = \left\{ \begin{matrix} \text{set of all outcomes } \omega \text{ such that} \\ X(\omega) \leqslant a \end{matrix} \right\}.$$

Given a rule which permits probability statements related to this class of events, all other probability statements concerning events associated with the random variable may be derived.

Definition 2.7: The function defined by

$$F: \quad F(a) = P\{X(\omega) \leqslant a\} \qquad (-\infty < a < \infty)$$
$$\text{(i.e.} \quad F(a) = P\{E_a\})$$

is called the *cumulative distribution function*, or just the *distribution function* (abbreviated c.d.f. or d.f.), of the random variable X.

In order to emphasize that the cumulative distribution function depends on the random variable under consideration, it may be denoted by F_X. The particular value taken by the function at a is $F_X(a)$.

If $a < b$ and if an event is of the form

$$E_{a,b} = \{a < X(\omega) \leqslant b\}$$

it can be seen that

$$E_a \cap E_{a,b} = \phi.$$

Hence, by the addition rule for probabilities,

$$P\{E_a \cup E_{a,b}\} = P\{E_a\} + P\{E_{a,b}\}.$$

However, $E_a \cup E_{a,b} = E_b,$

so that $P\{E_a \cup E_{a,b}\} = P\{E_b\} = F_X(b).$

Therefore,

$$F_X(b) = F_X(a) + P\{a < X(\omega) \leqslant b\}$$

and $P\{a < X(\omega) \leqslant b\} = F_X(b) - F_X(a).$

The cumulative distribution function has the following properties:

(1)   It is a non-decreasing function.

(2) $F_X(-\infty) = 0.$

(3) $F_X(\infty) = 1.$

It is important to remember that the domain of a cumulative distribution function is the set of all real numbers. Hence, in order to define a cumulative distribution function, one must give the value of this function for every element in the set of all real numbers.

When the random variable of interest is of the discrete type, it is convenient to speak of a *probability function*. If X is the random variable under study, the probability function of X will be denoted by P_X, where

$$P_X(k) = P\{X(\omega) = k\}.$$

Its domain is the range of X. The c.d.f. can be expressed as

$$F_X: \quad F_X(a) = \sum_{k \leqslant a} P_X(k) \quad (-\infty < a < \infty).$$

When the random variable is of the continuous type, we can usually write

$$P\{a < X(\omega) \leqslant b\} = F_X(b) - F_X(a)$$

in the form of an integral

$$\int_a^b f_X(t) \, dt \quad \text{for all } a \leqslant b,$$

i.e.
$$f_X(t) = \frac{dF_X(t)}{dt}.$$

Definition 2.8: If $F_X(a)$ can be expressed as an integral of the form

$$F_X(a) = \int_{-\infty}^a f_X(t) \, dt \qquad (-\infty < a < \infty)$$

then f_X is called the *density function* of the random variable X.

NOTE: (1) f_X must be non-negative (i.e. its range is restricted to the set of non-negative real numbers).

(2)
$$\int_{-\infty}^{\infty} f_X(t) \, dt = 1.$$

(3) $f_X(v)$ is *not* the probability that $X(\omega) = v$. In fact, this probability is

$$\int_v^v f_X(t) \, dt = 0.$$

Example 2.13: An experiment consists of producing a fountain pen. Assume that the probability of producing a defective pen is known to be equal to p. Suppose that a random variable, the gain to the producer, denoted by G, is defined as follows:

$$G: \quad G(\omega) = \left\{ \begin{array}{l} -\$1.00 \text{ if a defective pen is produced} \\ \ \ \$5.00 \text{ if a good pen is produced} \end{array} \right\}.$$

Then, the probability function of G is given by

$$P_G: \quad P_G(-\$1.00) = p,$$
$$P_G(\ \ \$5.00) = 1-p.$$

The c.d.f. of G is

$$\begin{aligned} F_G: \quad F_G(a) &= 0 & (-\infty < a < -\$1.00) \\ &= p & (\ \ \$1.00 \leqslant a < \$5.00) \\ &= 1 & (\$5.00 \leqslant a < \infty). \end{aligned}$$

Sometimes it is helpful to draw the graphs of the probability function and the cumulative distribution function. These are shown in Figures 1 and 2, which follow. The graph of the probability function is actually the set of points at the top of each of the lines illustrated in Figure 1. For obvious reasons, it is convenient to represent the function as a line graph of the type illustrated.

Example 2.14: An experiment consists of the production of an alloy steel ingot for nitriding purposes. Suppose that it is known that the percentage of carbon, denoted by C, in the ingot is a continuous random variable with a density function as given below.

$$\begin{aligned} f_C: \quad f_C(a) &= \ \ 5+200(a-0.20) & \text{if} \quad 0.20 \leqslant a < 0.25, \\ &= 15-200(a-0.25) & \text{if} \quad 0.25 \leqslant a \leqslant 0.30, \\ &= 0 & \text{otherwise.} \end{aligned}$$

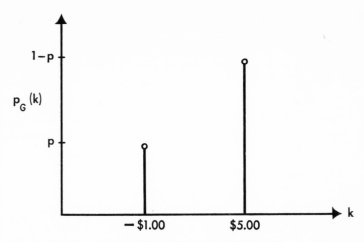

FIG. 1. Graphical representation of the probability function of a discrete random variable. (Example 2.13.)

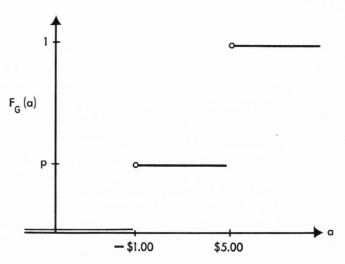

FIG. 2. Graphical representation of the cumulative distribution function of a discrete random variable. (Example 2.13.)

The graph of this density function is given in Figure 3.

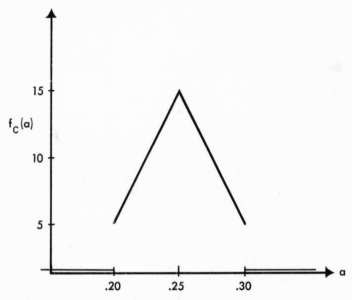

FIG. 3. Graph of the density function of a continuous random variable. (Example 2.14.)

The cumulative distribution function of C is obtained, as specified earlier, from the expression

$$F_C(b) = \int_{-\infty}^{b} f_C(a) \, da \quad (-\infty < b < \infty).$$

Hence, F_C:

$$F_C(b) = 0 \qquad\qquad\qquad\qquad (-\infty < b < 0 \cdot 20)$$

$$\left. \begin{aligned} &= 0 + \int_{0 \cdot 20}^{b} 5 + 200(a - 0 \cdot 20) \, da \\ &= 100b^2 - 35b + 3 \end{aligned} \right\} \quad (0 \cdot 20 \leqslant b < 0 \cdot 25)$$

$$= 0 + \tfrac{1}{2} + \int_{0\cdot25}^{b} 15 - 200(a - 0\cdot25)\, da \left.\right\} \ (0\cdot25 \leqslant b \leqslant 0\cdot30)$$
$$= 65b - 100b^2 - 9\cdot5$$
$$= 1 \qquad\qquad (0\cdot30 < b < \infty).$$

Figure 4 shows the graph of this cumulative distribution function.

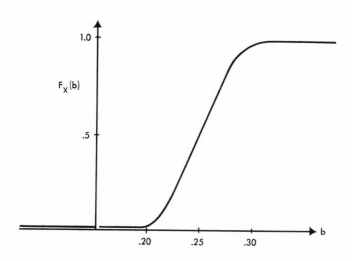

FIG. 4. Graph of the cumulative distribution function of a continuous random variable. (Example 2.14.)

EXERCISES—IV

1. A firm produces and classifies sweaters into five categories depending upon quality characteristics denoted by C_1, C_2,..., C_5.

Assume that it is known that the following probabilities can be associated with the event that a sweater produced falls into a particular category:

$$P\{C_1\} = \tfrac{5}{16} \qquad P\{C_4\} = \tfrac{1}{16}$$
$$P\{C_2\} = \tfrac{1}{4} \qquad P\{C_5\} = \tfrac{1}{8}.$$
$$P\{C_3\} = \tfrac{1}{4}$$

If A denotes the event $\{C_1 \cup C_3 \cup C_5\}$
$\quad$ B the event $\{C_1 \cup C_2 \cup C_4\}$
$\quad$ D the event $\{C_3 \cup C_4\}$
and E the event $\{C_2 \cup C_5\}$,

find:

$\quad$ (a) $P\{A\}$, $P\{B\}$, $P\{D\}$, $P\{E\}$.
$\quad$ (b) $P\{A \cup B\}$, $\quad P\{D \cup E\}$.
$\quad$ (c) $P\{A \cap B\}$.
$\quad$ (d) $P\{A \cup B \cup D \cup E\}$.
$\quad$ (e) $P\{A \cap B \cap D\}$.
$\quad$ (f) $P\{B \cap E\}$.
$\quad$ (g) $P\{A \cap D\}$.

If the firm obtains a profit of $\$1.00$ from each sweater in C_1
$\qquad\qquad\qquad\qquad\qquad$ $\$0.80$ from each sweater in C_2
$\qquad\qquad\qquad\qquad\qquad$ $\$0.60$ from each sweater in C_3
$\qquad\qquad\qquad\qquad\qquad$ $\$0.00$ from each sweater in C_4
$\qquad\qquad\qquad\qquad$ $-\$0.60$ from each sweater in C_5,

and if it produces 200,000 sweaters per year,

$\quad$ (h) assuming that the frequency interpretation of probability is reasonable for this situation, what might you expect the yearly profit to be?

$\quad$ (i) By spending $\$1,000$ each year, the firm can reduce the probability of event C_5 occurring by one-eighth and increase the probability of event C_1, occurring by one-eighth. Would you advise the firm to spend the $\$1,000$ each year?

2. A company makes shafts and cams. Each of these items is classified into five categories $(a_1, a_2, a_3, a_4, a_5)$. An experiment consists of pairing a cam and a shaft to be sent to a customer. For example, (a_5, a_2) denotes the outcome that the pair includes a shaft in category a_5 and a cam in category a_2. Assume that all outcomes have equal probability. Suppose that two random variables S (denoting the outside diameter, O.D., of a shaft) and C (denoting the inside diameter, I.D., of a cam) are of interest,

where

$$S: \quad S(a_i, a_j) = \begin{cases} 1\cdot01'' & \text{for } i = 1 \\ 1\cdot02'' & \text{for } i = 2 \\ 1\cdot03'' & \text{for } i = 3 \\ 1\cdot04'' & \text{for } i = 4 \\ 1\cdot05'' & \text{for } i = 5 \end{cases} \text{ and } j = 1,...,5 \Bigg\},$$

$$C: \quad C(a_i, a_j) = \begin{cases} 1\cdot01'' & \text{for } j = 1 \\ 1\cdot02'' & \text{for } j = 2 \\ 1\cdot03'' & \text{for } j = 3 \\ 1\cdot04'' & \text{for } j = 4 \\ 1\cdot05'' & \text{for } j = 5 \end{cases} \text{ and } i = 1,...,5 \Bigg\}.$$

Assume that the following random variables are also of interest:

$$D: \quad D(C, S) = C - S$$
$$R: \quad R(C, S) = \tfrac{1}{2}(C + S)$$
$$M: \quad M(C, S) = \text{maximum } (C, S).$$

(a) List the outcomes of the sample space in tabular form.
(b) In the same table list the values of each of the above random variables.
(c) In the same table list the values of the probability functions of the random variables D, R, and M.
(d) Describe the following cumulative distribution functions:

$$(1) \quad F_D, \qquad (2) \ F_R, \qquad (3) \ F_M.$$

(e) Those cam-shaft pairs which 'fit' can be classed in two categories: a *tight fit*, where the shaft and cam both have the same diameter, and a *loose fit*, where the shaft O.D. is exactly $0\cdot01''$ less than the cam I.D. All other pairs do not fit. Assume that the following events are of interest:

A = event that a pair gives a *tight* fit. $D = 0$

B = event that a pair does *not* fit.

C = event that one-half the sum of the O.D. of a shaft and I.D. of a cam is greater than or equal to $1\cdot04''$. $R = 1 \cdot 04$ or greater

$E = \{A \cap C\}$.

Find:

(1) $P\{A\}$,   (2) $P\{B\}$,   (3) $P\{C\}$,
(4) Which outcomes does event E include?   (5) $P\{E\}$.

Loose fit $= C - S = .01$

(f) The quality control manager wishes to decide whether or not to introduce a new system of fitting cams and shafts. This new system will reduce the probability of a pair not fitting to zero and will cost \$0.05/pair more than the present system. Under the present system, however, customers return all non-fitting pairs that they receive at a cost to the company of \$0.20/pair returned. Should the new system be introduced? (Assume the frequency interpretation applies.)

3. A small bakery has found that the volume of daily demand (V, in pounds) for fresh (less than one day old) bread can be described by the following density function:

$$f_V: \quad f_V(a) = \begin{cases} k(1-0\cdot01a) & \text{for } 0 \leqslant a \leqslant 100 \\ 0 & \text{otherwise} \end{cases}.$$

(a) Find k such that f_V is a density function.
(b) Describe the cumulative distribution function F_V.
(c) Suppose the bakery stocks 70 lb. of fresh bread each day. What is the probability of not satisfying demand on any given day? What is the probability of having surplus fresh bread on any given day?

4. The amount of oil (X) in thousands of gallons required to run a plant each day is a continuous random variable which has the following density function:

$$f_X: \quad f_X(a) = \begin{cases} 1 & \text{if } 0\cdot5 \leqslant a \leqslant 1 \\ 0\cdot5 & \text{if } 2 \leqslant a \leqslant 3 \\ 0 & \text{elsewhere} \end{cases}.$$

(a) Describe the cumulative distribution function F_X.

Compute:

(b) $P\{0\cdot75 < X \leqslant 1\}$.
(c) $P\{2\cdot5 < X \leqslant 3\}$.
(d) $P\{0\cdot75 < X \leqslant 2\cdot5\}$.
(e) If the plant storage tank could hold only 2,900 gallons of oil, what is the probability of a shortage on any day?

5. The density function of a continuous random variable is

$$f_X: \quad f_X(a) = \left\{ \begin{array}{ll} 0 & \text{for } a \leqslant 0 \\ \frac{1}{4} & \text{for } 0 < a \leqslant 1 \\ 0 & \text{for } 1 < a \leqslant 2 \\ \dfrac{a}{14} & \text{for } 2 < a \leqslant 5 \\ 0 & \text{for } 5 < a \end{array} \right\}.$$

(a) Describe the cumulative distribution function F_X.

Compute:

(b) $P\{\frac{1}{2} < X \leqslant \frac{3}{4}\}$.

(c) $P\{\frac{3}{4} < X \leqslant 4\}$.

2.5. *Distributions of special interest*

Listed below are some types of distributions for both discrete and continuous random variables which arise frequently in engineering problems.

TABLE I. *Distributions for some discrete random variables*

Type	Form of probability function	Parameters and conditions
Poisson distribution	$P(k) = \dfrac{e^{-\lambda}\lambda^k}{k!}$ $(k = 0, 1, ...)$	$\lambda > 0$
Binomial distribution	$P(k) = \dbinom{n}{k} p^k (1-p)^{n-k}$ $(k = 0, 1, ..., n)$	$n = 1, 2, ...$ $0 < p < 1$
Hypergeometric distribution	$P(k) = \dfrac{\dbinom{x}{k}\dbinom{N-x}{n-k}}{\dbinom{N}{n}}$ $(k = 0, 1, ..., n)$	$n, x, N = 1, 2, ...$ $x, n \leqslant N$

NOTE: $\dbinom{R}{S} = \dfrac{R(R-1)(R-2)...(R-S+1)}{S(S-1)(S-2)...(2)(1)} = \dfrac{R!}{S!(R-S)!}$.

TABLE II. *Distributions for some continuous random variables*

Type	Form of density function	Parameters and conditions
Normal distribution	$f(t) = \dfrac{1}{\sigma\sqrt{(2\pi)}}\, e^{-\frac{1}{2}[(t-\mu)/\sigma]^2}$ for $-\infty < t < \infty$	$-\infty < \mu < \infty$ $\sigma > 0$
Exponential distribution	$f(t) = \begin{cases} \theta e^{-\theta t} & \text{if } t \geqslant 0 \\ 0 & \text{if } t < 0 \end{cases}$	$\theta > 0$
Uniform distribution	$f(t) = \begin{cases} \dfrac{1}{b-a} & \text{if } a < t < b \\ 0 & \text{otherwise} \end{cases}$	$-\infty < a < b < \infty$
Chi-square distribution	$f(t) = \begin{cases} \dfrac{t^{\frac{1}{2}(\nu-2)}e^{-\frac{1}{2}t}}{2^{\frac{1}{2}\nu}\{\frac{1}{2}(\nu-2)\}!} & \\ & \text{if } t \geqslant 0 \\ 0 & \text{if } t < 0 \end{cases}$	$\nu = 1, 2, ...$ (called the *degrees of freedom*)
Student's t-distribution	$f(t) = \dfrac{\left(\dfrac{\nu-1}{2}\right)!\left(1+\dfrac{t^2}{\nu}\right)^{-\frac{1}{2}(\nu+1)}}{\left(\dfrac{\nu-2}{2}\right)!\sqrt{(\pi\nu)}}$ for $-\infty < t < \infty$	$\nu = 1, 2, ...$ (called the *degrees of freedom*)

If the parameters of the normal distribution have values of $\mu = 0$ and $\sigma = 1$, the distribution function is known as the *standard normal distribution* and is denoted by

$$\Phi: \quad \Phi(a) = \frac{1}{\sqrt{(2\pi)}} \int_{-\infty}^{a} e^{-\frac{1}{2}t^2}\, dt \quad (-\infty < a < \infty).$$

In order to obtain the probabilities of events related to normally distributed random variables, the cumulative distribution function

$$F_X: \quad F_X(a) = \int_{-\infty}^{a} \frac{1}{\sigma\sqrt{(2\pi)}} e^{-\frac{1}{2}[(t-\mu)/\sigma]^2} dt \quad (-\infty < a < \infty)$$

must be evaluated.

Since this integral cannot be evaluated exactly, it has been found convenient to tabulate values of the standard normal distribution function. See, for example, Table IV. Any integral of the above type may be put in this form by use of the transformation $z = (t-\mu)/\sigma$. This converts the above to

$$F_X: \quad F_X(a) = \int_{-\infty}^{\frac{a-\mu}{\sigma}} \frac{e^{-\frac{1}{2}z^2}}{\sqrt{(2\pi)}} dz = \Phi\left(\frac{a-\mu}{\sigma}\right).$$

That is, by appropriately changing the limits of integration, the tabulated values of the standard normal distribution can be used.

2.6. *Distributions of functions of random variables*

Frequently, the distribution of a *function* of a random variable X is of interest. If the distribution of X is known and if the function is denoted by G, the distribution of G, which is also a random variable, may be derived. In general, this is accomplished as follows:

By definition,

$$F_G: \quad F_G(a) = P\{G \leqslant a\} \quad (-\infty < a < \infty).$$

Hence, $\quad F_G(a) = P\{X \text{ is such that } G(X) \leqslant a\}.$

Example 2.15: Suppose that a random variable X has a normal distribution with parameters μ and σ and

$$G: \quad G(X) = \frac{X-\mu}{\sigma} \quad (-\infty < X < \infty).$$

Then,

$$F_G(a) = P\{G \leqslant a\} = P\left\{\frac{X-\mu}{\sigma} \leqslant a\right\}$$

$$= P\{X \leqslant a\sigma + \mu\} = F_X(a\sigma + \mu)$$

$$= \frac{1}{\sigma\sqrt{(2\pi)}} \int_{-\infty}^{a\sigma+\mu} e^{-\frac{1}{2}[(t-\mu)/\sigma]^2} \, dt = \frac{1}{\sqrt{(2\pi)}} \int_{-\infty}^{a} e^{-\frac{1}{2}z^2} \, dz$$

$$= \Phi(a) \qquad\qquad (-\infty < a < \infty)$$

by using the transformation

$$z = \frac{t-\mu}{\sigma}.$$

Thus, $G(X) = (X-\mu)/\sigma$ has a standard normal distribution.

It can be shown similarly that if G: $G(X) = cX + d$, where c and d are any constants (in the above $c = 1/\sigma$ and $d = -\mu/\sigma$), then G has a normal distribution with parameters $\mu' = c\mu + d$ and $\sigma'^2 = c^2\sigma^2$.

Example 2.16: Suppose that the random variable X has a standard normal distribution and

$$G: \quad G(X) = X^2 \quad (-\infty < X < \infty).$$

Then, if $a < 0$, $\qquad\qquad F_G(a) = 0$

since X^2 is never negative.

For values of $a \geqslant 0$

$$F_G(a) = P\{G \leqslant a\} = P\{X^2 \leqslant a\}$$

$$= P\{-\sqrt{a} \leqslant X \leqslant \sqrt{a}\} = \frac{1}{(2\pi)} \int_{-\sqrt{a}}^{\sqrt{a}} e^{-\frac{1}{2}t^2} \, dt$$

$$= \frac{2}{\sqrt{(2\pi)}} \int_{0}^{\sqrt{a}} e^{-\frac{1}{2}t^2} \, dt.$$

The density function is

$$f_G: \quad f_G(t) = 0 \qquad\qquad \text{if} \quad t < 0,$$

$$= \frac{dF_G(a)}{da}\bigg|_{a=t}$$

$$= \frac{1}{\sqrt{(2\pi t)}}\, e^{-\frac{1}{2}t} \qquad \text{if} \quad t \geqslant 0.$$

Example 2.17: Let D be a random variable denoting the distance between two bodies and suppose that

$$F_D: \quad F_D(a) = 0 \qquad\qquad (a \leqslant 0)$$

$$= 1 - e^{-a} \qquad\quad (a > 0).$$

Consider the random variable

$$G: \quad G(D) = \frac{K}{D^2} \qquad\qquad (D > 0)$$

which denotes the attractive force existing between the two bodies. K is a given positive constant.

Then,

$$F_G(a) = 0 \qquad\qquad\qquad \text{if} \quad a \leqslant 0,$$

$$= P\left\{\frac{K}{D^2} \leqslant a\right\} \qquad \text{if} \quad a > 0$$

$$= P\left\{D^2 \geqslant \frac{K}{a}\right\}$$

$$= P\left\{D \geqslant \sqrt{\frac{K}{a}}\right\}$$

$$= e^{-\sqrt{(K/a)}}.$$

Example 2.18: A Profilometer (an instrument used for measuring the surface roughness of metals) has been found to yield normally distributed errors from the true value when utilized for routine measurements of the finish of valve seat inserts for a certain engine. Suppose that the parameters of the distribution are $\mu = 1$ microinch rms and $\sigma = 1 \cdot 5$ microinches rms.

It is desired to know the probability that an absolute error occurs which is greater than 3 microinches rms. Let E denote the random variable (error). The distribution function of interest is $F_{|E|}$; more specifically, for the problem under consideration

$$P\{|E| > 3\} = 1 - F_{|E|}(3)$$
$$= P\{[E > 3] \cup [E < -3]\}$$
$$= P\{E > 3\} + P\{E < -3\}.$$

The computations follow, using the result of Example 2.15.

$$P\{E > 3\} = P\left\{\frac{E-\mu}{\sigma} > \frac{3-\mu}{\sigma}\right\} = P\left\{\frac{E-\mu}{\sigma} > \frac{3-1}{1 \cdot 5}\right\}$$

$$= \frac{1}{\sqrt{(2\pi)}} \int_{\frac{3-1}{1 \cdot 5}}^{\infty} e^{-\frac{1}{2}t^2} dt = 0 \cdot 092.$$

Similarly,

$$P\{E < -3\} = P\left\{\frac{E-\mu}{\sigma} < \frac{-3-1}{1 \cdot 5}\right\}$$

$$= \frac{1}{\sqrt{(2\pi)}} \int_{-\infty}^{\frac{-3-1}{1 \cdot 5}} e^{-\frac{1}{2}t^2} dt = 0 \cdot 004.$$

Consequently,

$$P\{|E| > 3\} = 0 \cdot 092 + 0 \cdot 004 = 0 \cdot 096.$$

EXERCISES—V

1. The number of orders per day (N) for Swiss watches was found by a retailer to have a Poisson distribution with parameter $\lambda = 6$.

   (a) Find:

      (1) $P\{1 < N < 4\}$.   (4) $P\{N > 6\}$.

      (2) $P\{1 \leqslant N < 4\}$.   (5) $P\{N \geqslant 6\}$.

      (3) $P\{N = 6\}$.   (6) $P\{1 \leqslant N \leqslant 4\}$.

   (b) The retailer stocks enough watches to fill eight orders per day. What is the probability on a given day that he will have a shortage?

   (c) The cost of changing the parameter to a new value λ' is given by $C(\lambda') = (6-\lambda')^2$. What is the cost of reducing the probability of a shortage based on stocking policy in part (b) by $0 \cdot 01$?
    Hint: Use tables.

2. The number of customers (N) arriving at a store each day has a Poisson distribution with parameter $\lambda = 5$.
Find:

   (a) $P\{N > 5\}$.   (d) $P\{N \leqslant 5\}$.

   (b) $P\{N < 3\}$.   (e) $P\{N > 3\}$.

   (c) $P\{N = 3\}$.   (f) $P\{N = 0\}$.

3. The number of oil tankers (N) arriving at a certain refinery each day has been found to have a Poisson distribution with parameter $\lambda = 2$. Present port facilities can service three tankers a day. If more than three tankers arrive in a day, the tankers in excess of three must be sent to another port.

   (a) What is the probability, on a given day, of having to send any tankers away?

   (b) How much must present facilities be increased to enable handling all arriving tankers on approximately 99 per cent of the days?

4. Each cam-shaft pair which is sent to a customer is either acceptable or not acceptable. The probability that a pair is acceptable is $0 \cdot 75$ (i.e. $p = 0 \cdot 75$). If a customer receives three (i.e. $n = 3$)

cam-shaft pairs, find the probability that the number (N) of acceptable cam-shaft pairs is:

  (a) zero,
  (b) one,
  (c) less than or equal to two,
  (d) three.

  (Hint: Assume that the random variable (N) has a binomial distribution.)

5. The length of life in months of a certain vacuum tube used in radar sets has been found to be exponentially distributed with parameter $\theta = 2$. If a tube fails, the radar set is inoperable. If a new tube is put in at the end of every month, what is the probability in any given month of failure before replacement?

6. It has been found that the amount (X) of regular octane gasoline to be stored in the tanks of an oil refinery at the start of each day has a distribution which is approximately normal with parameter $\mu = 10$ (million) and $\sigma = 2$ (million). Each tank holds 0·1 (million) gallons.

  (a) Compute:

    (1) $P\{10 < X \leqslant 16\}$.
    (2) $P\{8 < X \leqslant 12\}$.
    (3) $P\{8 < X \leqslant 10\}$.

  (b) How many tanks should the refinery have so that the probability of exceeding its capacity at the start of any day is less than 0·01?

7. When a salesman places an order for delivery of foam-rubber mattresses to a customer, the lag in weeks between ordering and delivering of the goods is called 'lead time.' A company has found that the 'lead time' (X) for its mattresses is normally distributed with $\mu = 6$ and $\sigma = 2$.

  (a) Find:

    (1) $P\{8 < X \leqslant 9\}$.
    (2) $P\{0 < X \leqslant 7\}$.
    (3) $P\{2 < X \leqslant 6\}$.

(b) Management has experienced a considerable cost of lost business when customers have been forced to wait six weeks or more for delivery. What is the probability that such an event occurs?

(c) The cost in thousands of dollars of changing the parameter μ to a new value denoted by μ' is given by the formula $c(\mu') = (4 - \mu')$. What will be the cost of changing μ to a new value such that the probability that a customer must wait six weeks or more for delivery is reduced to 0.01?

8. It is known that a bolt manufacturing process has the property that the diameter of a bolt is a random variable having a normal distribution with parameter $\mu = 0.25$ and $\sigma^2 = 0.0001$. Bolt specifications call for diameters of 0.24 ± 0.02. What is the probability of producing a defective bolt?

2.7. *Some descriptive properties of distributions*

It has been found satisfactory for most engineering purposes to focus on the properties of distribution functions given below.

Definition 2.9: The value of a such that

$$F_X(a) = \alpha$$

is called the 100α *percentile* of the distribution of the random variable X.

Note that in the case of discrete random variables, the 100α percentile, for every α, will not always exist as defined.

Definition 2.10: The *median* is the value a such that $\alpha = \frac{1}{2}$. The median describes, to some extent, the location of the center of a distribution.

Definition 2.11: If a_2 is the 75th percentile and a_1 the 25th percentile, the difference $(a_2 - a_1)$ is called the *interquartile range*.

The interquartile range is sometimes useful as a measure of spread of the distribution.

Definition 2.12: The *mode*, sometimes called the *most probable value*, is the value of a such that:

    (1) if a density function exists, $f_X(a)$ is a maximum;

    (2) if a probability function exists, $P_X(a)$ is a maximum.

The mode is sometimes used as a centrality measure.

Example 2.19: The density function of a random variable X is:

$$f_X: \quad f_X(a) = \tfrac{1}{2}a \qquad (0 \leqslant a \leqslant 1)$$

$$= \tfrac{1}{4} \qquad (1 < a \leqslant 4)$$

$$= 0 \qquad \text{(otherwise).}$$

It is easily confirmed that the median is equal to 2, the mode is equal to 1, and the interquartile range is equal to 2.

Definition 2.13: The *expected value* (or the *mean*) of a random variable X (denoted by EX) is defined as follows:

    (1) For a continuous random variable

$$EX = \int\limits_{-\infty}^{\infty} af_X(a)\,da.$$

    (2) For a discrete random variable

$$EX = \sum_{\substack{\text{over all} \\ a}} aP_X(a).$$

It is the most frequently used measure of centrality of a distribution. Note the relationship with well-known expressions for the determination of the center of gravity of a mass distributed continuously over a weightless bar for the first case, and for the second case that used for the computation of the center of moments of a system of isolated parallel forces distributed along a line. The statistical significance of the expected value will become apparent in a later section dealing with the 'law of large numbers.'

Example 2.20: If a random variable X has an exponential distribution with parameter $\theta = 1$, i.e.

$$f_X: \quad f_X(a) = e^{-a} \qquad\qquad (a \geqslant 0)$$
$$= 0 \qquad\qquad (a < 0),$$

then
$$EX = \int_{-\infty}^{\infty} a f_X(a)\, da = \int_0^{\infty} a e^{-a}\, da = 1.$$

Example 2.21: A process used for producing batteries is such that the probability of producing a defective item is known to be 0.02. If a random variable, the profit, is

$$X: \quad X \text{ (defective)} = -\$0.10,$$
$$X \text{ (non-defective)} = \$0.03,$$

then
$$P_X: \quad P_X(-\$0.10) = 0.02$$
$$P_X(\$0.03) \quad = 0.98.$$

The expected profit from the process (i.e. from the production of one battery) is given by:

$$EX = (-0.10)0.02 + (0.03)0.98 = \$0.027.$$

Example 2.22: If a random variable X is normally distributed with parameters μ, σ, then

$$EX = \int_{-\infty}^{\infty} \frac{a}{\sigma\sqrt{(2\pi)}}\, e^{-\frac{1}{2}[(a-\mu)/\sigma]^2}\, da.$$

Let $z = (a - \mu)/\sigma$, $dz = da/\sigma$, then

$$EX = \int_{-\infty}^{\infty} \frac{\mu + z}{\sqrt{(2\pi)}} e^{-\frac{1}{2}z^2} dz$$

$$= \frac{1}{\sqrt{(2\pi)}} \int_{-\infty}^{\infty} \mu e^{-\frac{1}{2}z^2} dz + \frac{1}{\sqrt{(2\pi)}} \int_{-\infty}^{\infty} z e^{-\frac{1}{2}z^2} dz = \mu.$$

It is often necessary to compute the expected value of a function of a random variable. One method of accomplishing this would be to derive the distribution function of this new random variable and then to apply Definition 2.13; i.e. if the new random variable is G and the original random variable is X, then

$$EG = \left\{ \begin{array}{ll} \int_{-\infty}^{\infty} a f_G(a)\, da & \text{if} \quad G \text{ is continuous} \\ \sum_a a P_G(a) & \text{if} \quad G \text{ is discrete} \end{array} \right\}.$$

However, it is usually easier to make the computation by *Definition* 2.14:

$$EG = \left\{ \begin{array}{ll} \int_{-\infty}^{\infty} G(a) f_X(a)\, da & \text{if} \quad X \text{ is continuous} \\ \sum_a G(a) P_X(a) & \text{if} \quad X \text{ is discrete} \end{array} \right\}.$$

It can be shown that the two methods of evaluation lead to the same result.

Example 2.23: Suppose X is as in Example 2.20, above, and G: $G(x) = X + 10$, then

$$EG = \int_{-\infty}^{\infty} (a + 10) f_X(a)\, da = \int_{0}^{\infty} (a + 10) e^{-a}\, da$$

$$= \int\limits_0^\infty ae^{-a}\,da + \int\limits_0^\infty 10e^{-a}\,da = 1 + 10 = 11.$$

On the other hand, if the distribution function of G is first derived as follows:

$$F_G(a) = P\{G \leqslant a\} = P\{X + 10 \leqslant a\}$$
$$= P\{X \leqslant (a-10)\} = F_X(a-10),$$

then
$$F_G(a) = 1 - e^{-(a-10)} \qquad (a \geqslant 10)$$

$$f_G(a) = e^{-(a-10)} \qquad (a \geqslant 10)$$

and both $\qquad F_G(a) = f_G(a) = 0 \qquad\qquad (a < 10).$

By Definition 2.13

$$EG = \int\limits_{-\infty}^\infty a f_G(a)\,da = \int\limits_{10}^\infty ae^{-(a-10)}\,da.$$

If $t = a - 10$, this becomes

$$= \int\limits_0^\infty (t+10)e^{-t}\,dt = 11.$$

Example 2.24: A random variable X has a distribution such that $P_X(0) = 1-p$ and $P_X(1) = p$. Of interest is another random variable G: $G(X) = 5X^2 + 3$. By the above,

$$EG = [5(0)^2+3]P_X(0) + [5(1)^2+3]P_X(1)$$
$$= 3(1-p) + 8p = 5p + 3.$$

To evaluate EG directly, note that $P_X(0) = P_G(3) = 1-p$ and $P_X(1) = P_G(8) = p$. Hence

$$EG = 3P_G(3) + 8P_G(8) = 5p + 3.$$

Definition 2.15: If
$$G: \quad G(X) = (X-c)^k,$$
then $EG = E(X-c)^k$ is called the *k-th moment* of the distribution (or of the random variable X) about the constant c.

Definition 2.16: An important case of the above is that of $k = 2$, $c = EX$. Under these circumstances $E(X-EX)^2$ is called the *variance* of the distribution of X and is denoted by Var X. The variance, to some extent, describes the dispersion of the distribution about the mean.

NOTE: Similar to the equivalence of Definitions 2.13 and 2.14, if Z is a function of X and if both are continuous,

$$\text{Var } Z = E(Z-EZ)^2 = \int_{-\infty}^{\infty} (a-EZ)^2 f_Z(a) \, da$$

or $$\text{Var } Z = \int_{-\infty}^{\infty} [Z(a)-EZ]^2 f_X(a) \, da.$$

If both are discrete,

$$\text{Var } Z = \sum_a (a-EZ)^2 P_Z(a)$$

or $$\text{Var } Z = \sum_a [Z(a)-EZ]^2 P_X(a).$$

Definition 2.17: The quantity $\sigma_X = \sqrt{(\text{Var } X)}$ is called the *standard deviation* of the distribution of X. The standard deviation is usually used as a measure of the dispersion in preference to the variance because the physical units of the standard deviation are the same as those of the mean, while those of the variance are squared.

Example 2.25: A random variable X has the distribution given in Example 2.24 with $p = \frac{1}{5}$. Suppose that a random variable R is of interest, where $R: R(X) = \frac{1}{3}X$.

Then
$$ER = \frac{1}{3}P_X(1) + 0P_X(0) = \frac{1}{3} \cdot \frac{1}{5} = \frac{1}{15}$$

$$\text{Var } R = \left(0 - \frac{1}{15}\right)^2 P_X(0) + \left(\frac{1}{3} - \frac{1}{15}\right)^2 P_X(1)$$

$$= \left(\frac{-1}{15}\right)^2 \frac{4}{5} + \left(\frac{4}{15}\right)^2 \frac{1}{5} = \frac{4}{225},$$

and $\sigma_R = \frac{2}{15}$.

Example 2.26: The density function of a random variable X is uniform over the interval $(-1, 1)$, i.e.

$$f_X: \quad f_X(a) = \tfrac{1}{2} \quad \text{if} \quad -1 \leqslant a \leqslant 1$$
$$= 0 \quad \text{otherwise.}$$

Then $EX = 0$, and

$$\text{Var } X = \int_{-\infty}^{\infty} (a - EX)^2 f_X(a)\, da = \frac{1}{2} \int_{-1}^{1} a^2\, da = \frac{a^3}{6}\bigg|_{-1}^{1} = \frac{1}{3}.$$

If a new random variable is given by $G: G(X) = 2X + 4$, then, to apply Definition 2.13, the distribution function of G is first derived:

$$F_G(a) = P\{G \leqslant a\} = P\{2X + 4 \leqslant a\}$$
$$= P\left\{X \leqslant \frac{a-4}{2}\right\} = F_X\left(\frac{a-4}{2}\right).$$

Therefore,

$$F_G: \quad F_G(a) = 0 \qquad\qquad\qquad (a < 2)$$
$$= \frac{1}{2}\left(\frac{a-4}{2}\right) + \frac{1}{2} = \frac{1}{2} + \frac{a-4}{4} \quad (2 \leqslant a \leqslant 6)$$
$$= 1 \qquad\qquad\qquad (6 < a)$$

and

$$f_G: \quad f_G(a) = \tfrac{1}{4} \qquad\qquad (2 \leqslant a \leqslant 6)$$
$$= 0 \qquad\qquad\qquad \text{(otherwise).}$$

By the symmetry of f_G it is clear that $EG = 4$. Hence, by Definition 2.14,

$$\text{Var } G = \int_{-\infty}^{\infty} [(2a+4)-4]^2 \tfrac{1}{2} \, da$$

$$= \int_{-1}^{1} 2a^2 \, da = 2\left[\frac{a^3}{3}\right]_{-1}^{1} = 1\tfrac{1}{3}.$$

Using Definition 2.13,

$$\text{Var } G = \int_{-\infty}^{\infty} (a-4)^2 \tfrac{1}{4} \, da = 1\tfrac{1}{3}.$$

Of special interest are the following (proofs are omitted):

(1) If X has a normal distribution with parameters μ and σ, then

$$EX = \int_{-\infty}^{\infty} \frac{te^{-\frac{1}{2}[(t-\mu)/\sigma]^2}}{\sigma\sqrt{2\pi}} \, dt = \mu$$

and
$$\text{Var } X = \int_{-\infty}^{\infty} (t-\mu)^2 \frac{e^{-\frac{1}{2}[(t-\mu)/\sigma]^2}}{\sigma\sqrt{2\pi}} = \sigma^2.$$

(2) If X has a Poisson distribution with parameter λ, then

$$EX = \sum_{k=0}^{\infty} k \frac{e^{-\lambda}\lambda^k}{k!} = \lambda$$

and
$$\text{Var } X = \sum_{k=0}^{\infty} (k-\lambda)^2 \frac{e^{-\lambda}\lambda^k}{k!} = \lambda.$$

(3) If X has a binomial distribution with parameters n and p, then

$$EX = \sum_{k=0}^{n} k \binom{n}{k} p^k (1-p)^{n-k} = np$$

and

$$\text{Var}\, X = \sum_{k=0}^{n} (k-np)^2 \binom{n}{k} p^k (1-p)^{n-k} = np(1-p).$$

Example 2.27: A standard process is used for the production of shear pins, which are utilized in outboard motors. It is known that a pin so produced has length, denoted by X, which is approximately normally distributed with mean $\mu = 1\cdot00$ inches and standard deviation $\sigma = 0\cdot02$ inches. Specifications for the pin call for items which fall within $1\cdot00 \pm 0\cdot04$ inches. If a pin is too long it can be reworked to meet the specifications, giving rise, when sold, to a profit of 2 cents. If a pin is too short it is sold for scrap; this results in an eventual loss of 1 cent. If a pin meets the specifications, it may be sold at a profit to the firm of 5 cents. It is of interest to compute the expected profit and the standard deviation of the profit from the manufacture of shear pins using the given process.

Since X is normal, the probability of producing pins in the various categories is given by

$$P\{\text{short pin}\} = P\{X < 0\cdot96\}$$

$$= \frac{1}{\sqrt{(2\pi)}} \int\limits_{-\infty}^{\frac{0\cdot96-1\cdot00}{0\cdot02}} e^{-\frac{1}{2}t^2}\, dt = 0\cdot023,$$

$$P\{\text{good pin}\} = P\{0\cdot96 \leqslant X \leqslant 1\cdot04\}$$

$$= \frac{1}{\sqrt{(2\pi)}} \int\limits_{\frac{0\cdot96-1\cdot00}{0\cdot02}}^{\frac{1\cdot04-1\cdot00}{0\cdot02}} e^{-\frac{1}{2}t^2}\, dt = 0\cdot954,$$

$$P\{\text{long pin}\} = P\{X > 1 \cdot 04\}$$

$$= \frac{1}{\sqrt{(2\pi)}} \int_{\frac{1 \cdot 04 - 1 \cdot 00}{0 \cdot 02}}^{\infty} e^{-\frac{1}{2}t^2} \, dt = 0 \cdot 023.$$

If G is used to denote the random variable, profit, its probability function is

$$P_G: \quad P_G(-1) = 0 \cdot 023$$
$$P_G(5) = 0 \cdot 954$$
$$P_G(2) = 0 \cdot 023.$$

Hence, the expected profit is

$$EG = (-1)0 \cdot 023 + 5(0 \cdot 954) + 2(0 \cdot 023) = 4 \cdot 79 \text{ cents}$$

and the standard deviation of the profit is

$$\sigma_G = [(-1 \cdot 00 - 4 \cdot 79)^2 0 \cdot 023 + (5 \cdot 00 - 4 \cdot 79)^2 \, 0 \cdot 954 +$$
$$+ (2 \cdot 00 - 4 \cdot 79)^2 \, 0 \cdot 023]^{\frac{1}{2}} = 0 \cdot 996.$$

Listed in Table III is a summary of the expected values and variances of random variables having the distribution functions described in Tables I and II.

TABLE III. *The expected values and variances of some important distributions*

Distribution	Expected value	Variance
Poisson . . .	λ	λ
Binomial . . .	np	$np(1-p)$
Hypergeometric .	nx/N	$\left(\dfrac{N-n}{N-1}\right)\dfrac{nx}{N}\left(1-\dfrac{x}{N}\right)$
Normal . . .	μ	σ^2
Exponential . .	$1/\theta$	$1/\theta^2$
Uniform . . .	$\frac{1}{2}(a+b)$	$\frac{1}{12}(b-a)^2$
Chi-square . .	ν	2ν
Student's t . .	0	$\dfrac{\nu}{\nu-2}$ for $\nu > 2$

An important property of expected values which follows immediately from the definition is

Theorem 1: If c is an arbitrary constant, then

$$E(cX)^k = c^k EX^k.$$

Also easy to obtain directly is

Theorem 2: If c is an arbitrary constant, then

$$\text{Var}(cX) = c^2 \text{Var } X$$

and

$$\sigma_{cX} = c\sigma_X.$$

2.7.1. CHEBYSHEV'S INEQUALITY

If the density function of a continuous random variable X is known, an exact expression for $P\{|X-EX| > c\}$ is given by

$$\int\limits_{|t-EX|>c} f_X(t) \, dt = \int\limits_{-\infty}^{EX-c} f_X(t) \, dt + \int\limits_{EX+c}^{\infty} f_X(t) \, dt.$$

If the density function is unknown, an exact computation is no longer possible. However, if the variance is known, an *upper bound* for the probability of the event $\{|X-EX| > c\}$ can be obtained. This is given by the following expression (called *Chebyshev's inequality*):

$$P\{|X-EX| > c\} \leqslant \frac{\text{Var } X}{c^2} \qquad (c > 0).$$

Proof:

$$\text{Var } X = \int\limits_{-\infty}^{\infty} (t-EX)^2 f_X(t) \, dt$$

$$\geqslant \int\limits_{-\infty}^{EX-c} (t-EX)^2 f_X(t) \, dt + \int\limits_{EX+c}^{\infty} (t-EX)^2 f_X(t) \, dt$$

$$\geqslant \int\limits_{-\infty}^{EX-c} c^2 f_X(t) \, dt + \int\limits_{EX+c}^{\infty} c^2 f_X(t) \, dt$$

$$\geqslant c^2 P\{X < EX-c\}+P\{X > EX+c\}$$
$$\geqslant c^2 P\{|X-EX| > c\}.$$

Dividing through by c^2 yields the inequality. An analogous proof holds for the case in which X is discrete.

EXERCISES—VI

1. A manufacturer must decide which of two processes to use in producing a certain product. With process 1 the probability of producing a defective item is $0 \cdot 10$; with process 2 the probability of a defective item is $0 \cdot 05$. The cost to produce an item by process 1 is \$2.00. The cost for process 2 is \$3.00. A defective item cannot be sold. A non-defective item sells for \$4.00.

    (a) Which process should the manufacturer use in order to maximize his expected profit?

    (b) Compute the standard deviation of the profit for each process.

2. A machine has been set to cut wire rod to a specified length. The owner of this machine has found that a characteristic of the machine is that the difference between the cut-off length and the setting is a random variable which is normally distributed with expected value $= 0$ and standard deviation equal to $0 \cdot 05$ inches.

    Denote the difference between the specified (set) length and the actual cut-off length by D and assume the following schedule of *losses*:

$$L: \quad L(D) = \begin{cases} \$0.08 & \text{if } D < -0 \cdot 10 \\ \$0.30 & \text{if } -0 \cdot 10 \leqslant D \leqslant 0 \cdot 13 \\ \$0.08 & \text{if } D > 0 \cdot 13 \end{cases}.$$

Find:

    (a) $P_L(0 \cdot 08)$.

    (b) $P_L(-0 \cdot 30)$.

    (c) Describe F_L.

    (d) Compute EL, σ_L.

3. A random variable X is known to have the following density function:

$$f_X: \quad f_X(a) = \begin{cases} \tfrac{3}{4} & \text{if } -1 \leqslant a < 0 \\ \tfrac{1}{2}a & \text{if } 0 \leqslant a \leqslant 1 \\ 0 & \text{otherwise} \end{cases}.$$

(a) Compute EX.

(b) Compute σ_X.

(c) Compute the median of X.

(d) $P\{-\frac{1}{4} < X \leqslant \frac{1}{2}\}$.

If a function is defined as follows:

$$L: \quad L(X) = \left\{ \begin{array}{rl} 10 & \text{if } X < -\frac{1}{2} \\ -50 & \text{if } -\frac{1}{2} \leqslant X \leqslant \frac{1}{2} \\ 20 & \text{if } \frac{1}{2} < X \end{array} \right\}.$$

Describe

(e) F_L.

Compute

(f) EL.

(g) The mode of L.

(h) $P\{0 < L \leqslant 15\}$.

4. (a) Prove Theorems 1 and 2 for the case in which the random variable is continuous.

(b) Repeat (a) for a discrete random variable.

5. The density function of a random variable, Y, is:

$$f_Y: \quad f_Y(a) = \left\{ \begin{array}{ll} \frac{1}{4}a & \text{if } 0 < a \leqslant 2 \\ \frac{1}{2} & \text{if } 2 < a \leqslant 3 \\ 0 & \text{otherwise} \end{array} \right\}.$$

(a) Describe F_Y.

Compute:

(b) EY.

(c) σ_Y.

(d) Mode of Y.

(e) Median of Y.

(f) $P\{Y \leqslant 0\cdot9\}$.

(g) $P\{1\cdot3 < Y \leqslant 2\cdot5\}$.

Suppose that a random variable of interest is G: $\quad G(Y) = Y^2$.

(h) Describe F_G.

Compute:

(i) EG.

(j) σ_G.

(k) $P\{G \leqslant 0\cdot81\}$.

6. A small bakery has found that the daily demand (V) for fresh (less than one day old) bread can be described by the density function:

$$f_V: \quad f_V(a) = \begin{cases} 0.02(1-0.01a) & \text{if } 0 \leqslant a \leqslant 100 \text{ lb.} \\ 0 & \text{otherwise} \end{cases}.$$

The profit per pound of fresh bread sold is \$0.10. If bread is not sold on the day it is baked, it can be sold in unlimited quantities on the next day at a loss of \$0.05/lb. Assume that the demand for fresh bread is not affected by the amount of day-old bread sold. The bakery wishes to decide how much bread (b) to bake each day to maximize expected profits.

    (a) What is the expected daily demand? Median daily demand?

    (b) What is the variance of daily demand? Standard deviation of daily demand?

    (d) What is the expected quantity of daily sales?

    (d) What is the expected quantity of lost daily sales, i.e. unsatisfied demand?

    (e) What is the expected daily profit from baking (b) pounds of bread?

    (f) How many pounds of bread (b) should be baked to maximize expected daily profits?

7. The number of oil tankers (N) arriving at a certain refinery each day has a Poisson distribution with parameter $\lambda = 2$. Present port facilities can service three tankers a day. If more than three tankers arrive in a day, the tankers in excess of three must be sent to another port at a cost of \$2,000 per tanker sent away.

    (a) Prove that the expected value and the variance of the number of daily tanker arrivals are both equal to two.

    (b) What is the most probable number of daily tanker arrivals?

    (c) What is the expected number of tankers serviced daily?

    (d) What is the expected number of tankers turned away daily?

    (e) For an investment of \$200,000 the port facilities can be expanded to service four tankers daily. What is the new

        (1) expected number of tankers serviced daily?

        (2) expected number of tankers turned away daily?

8. The length of life (L) in months of a certain vacuum tube used in radar sets has been found to be exponentially distributed with parameter $\theta = 2$. In carrying out its preventative maintenance program, a company wishes to decide how many months (m) after installation a tube should be replaced to minimize the expected costs per tube. The cost per tube in dollars is denoted by C. The shortest practicable elapsed time between installation and replacement is $0 \cdot 01$ month. Subject to this restriction, what value of (m) minimizes EC in each of the following situations?

(a) if $C(L, m) = 3|L - m|$;

(b) if $C(L, m) = \begin{cases} 3 & \text{if } L < m \\ 5(L-m) & \text{if } m \leqslant L \end{cases}$;

(c) if $C(L, m) = \begin{cases} 2 & \text{if } L < m \\ 5(L-m) & \text{if } m \leqslant L \end{cases}$.

2.8. *Joint distribution functions*

In many engineering problems there is a simultaneous interest in more than one random variable defined over the sample space. For example, an experiment could consist of producing a gallon of diesel fuel oil by a standard process. A list of some of the potential random variables of interest could include:

X_1. Boiling-point.

X_2. Carbon residue.

X_3. Viscosity.

X_4. Water and sediment content.

X_5. Pour-point.

X_6. Flash-point.

X_7. Sulphur content.

X_8. Alkali and mineral acid content.

Typically, one could be interested in knowledge of the probability associated with joint events such as

$$E = \{a < X_3 \leqslant b \text{ and } c < X_5 \leqslant d\}.$$

The following extension of concepts previously developed for one random variable will enable probabilities of the occurrence of events such as E to be computed.

Let X_1 and X_2 be two random variables defined over the same sample space. Let E_a^1 denote the event $\{X_1 \leqslant a\}$ and E_b^2 be the event $\{X_2 \leqslant b\}$.

Definition 2.18: The *joint (cumulative) distribution function* of the random variables X_1 and X_2 is defined by

$$F_{X_1 X_2}: \quad F_{X_1 X_2}(a,b) = P\{X_1 \leqslant a \text{ and } X_2 \leqslant b\}$$
$$= P\{E_a^1 \cap E_b^2\}$$

where $-\infty < a < \infty$ and $-\infty < b < \infty$.

NOTE: (1) $\quad F_{X_1 X_2}(a, \infty) = P\{X_1 \leqslant a, X_2 \leqslant \infty\}$
$$= P\{E_a^1\} = P\{X_1 \leqslant a\}$$
$$= F_{X_1}(a).$$

(2) $\quad F_{X_1 X_2}(\infty, b) = F_{X_2}(b).$

(3) $F_{X_1 X_2}(-\infty, b) = F_{X_1 X_2}(a, -\infty) = P\{\phi\} = 0.$

The probability of events of the type

$$E = \{a_1 < X_1 \leqslant a_2, \, b_1 < X_2 \leqslant b_2\}$$

may now be computed if $F_{X_1 X_2}$ is known. For example,

$$P\{E\} = F_{X_1 X_2}(a_2, b_2) - F_{X_1 X_2}(a_2, b_1) - $$
$$- F_{X_1 X_2}(a_1, b_2) + F_{X_1 X_2}(a_1, b_1).$$

If X_1 and X_2 are discrete random variables, the joint distribution function is given by:

$$F_{X_1 X_2}: \quad F_{X_1 X_2}(a,b) = \sum_{r \leqslant a} \sum_{s \leqslant b} P_{X_1 X_2}(r, s)$$

where $-\infty < a < \infty$ and $-\infty < b < \infty$.

$P_{X_1 X_2}(r, s) = P\{X_1 = r, X_2 = s\}$ is called the *joint probability function* of X_1 and X_2.

Example 2.28: An experiment consists of the production of carbon steel castings. Four different grades $(\omega_1, ..., \omega_4)$ are produced with known probabilities:

$$P\{\omega_1\} = \tfrac{1}{4}, \quad P\{\omega_2\} = \tfrac{1}{2}, \quad P\{\omega_3\} = \tfrac{1}{8}, \quad P\{\omega_4\} = \tfrac{1}{8}.$$

The grades are characterized by the tensile strength (T) and the yield point (Y) as follows:

$$T: \quad T(\omega_1) = 45{,}000 \text{ psi} \qquad Y: \quad Y(\omega_1) = 15{,}000 \text{ psi}$$
$$T(\omega_2) = 50{,}000 \text{ psi} \qquad\qquad Y(\omega_2) = 18{,}000 \text{ psi}$$
$$T(\omega_3) = 45{,}000 \text{ psi} \qquad\qquad Y(\omega_3) = 18{,}000 \text{ psi}$$
$$T(\omega_4) = 50{,}000 \text{ psi} \qquad\qquad Y(\omega_4) = 20{,}000 \text{ psi}.$$

Hence, the joint probability function of T and Y is

$$P_{TY}: \quad P_{TY}(45{,}000, 15{,}000) = \tfrac{1}{4}$$
$$P_{TY}(45{,}000, 18{,}000) = \tfrac{1}{8}$$
$$P_{TY}(50{,}000, 18{,}000) = \tfrac{1}{2}$$
$$P_{TY}(50{,}000, 20{,}000) = \tfrac{1}{8}.$$

The process of describing the joint distribution function of T and Y is facilitated by locating the points having positive probability on the coordinate system shown in Figure 5, with the joint probabilities attached to each of the appropriate points.

The numbered sections in Figure 5 contain points in the domain of the joint distribution function, all of which give rise to the same value in the range of the function.

The joint distribution function is

$$F_{TY}: \quad F_{TY}(a, b)$$

		Section shown in Figure 5
$= 0$	$(a < 45{,}000, \quad b < 15{,}000)$	(1)
$= 0$	$(45{,}000 \leqslant a, \quad b < 15{,}000)$	(2)
$= 0$	$(a < 45{,}000, \quad 15{,}000 \leqslant b)$	(3)
$= \tfrac{1}{4}$	$(45{,}000 \leqslant a, \quad 15{,}000 \leqslant b < 18{,}000)$	(4)

$$= \tfrac{3}{8} \quad (45{,}000 \leqslant a < 50{,}000, \quad 18{,}000 \leqslant b) \quad (5)$$
$$= \tfrac{7}{8} \quad (50{,}000 \leqslant a, \quad 18{,}000 \leqslant b < 20{,}000) \quad (6)$$
$$= 1 \quad (50{,}000 \leqslant a, \quad 20{,}000 \leqslant b) \quad (7)$$

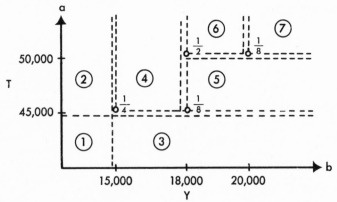

Fig. 5. View of the joint probability function of Example 2.29.

If $E = \{43{,}000 < T \leqslant 52{,}000, \; 16{,}000 < Y \leqslant 19{,}000\}$

$P\{E\} = F_{TY}(52{,}000, 19{,}000) - F_{TY}(52{,}000, 16{,}000) -$

$\qquad\qquad - F_{TY}(43{,}000, 19{,}000) + F_{TY}(43{,}000, 16{,}000)$

$P\{E\} = \tfrac{7}{8} - \tfrac{1}{4} - 0 + 0 = \tfrac{5}{8}.$

Definition 2.19: If $F_{X_1 X_2}(a, b)$ can be expressed as an integral of the form

$$\int\limits_{-\infty}^{b} \int\limits_{-\infty}^{a} f_{X_1 X_2}(u, v) \, du \, dv$$

for every value of a and b, then

$$f_{X_1 X_2}(u, v) = \frac{\partial^2 F_{X_1 X_2}(a, b)}{\partial a \, \partial b}\bigg|_{u, v}$$

is called the *joint density function* of the random variables X_1 and X_2.

In such a case

$$P\{a_1 < X_1 \leqslant a_2, b_1 < X_2 \leqslant b_2\} = \int\limits_{b_1}^{b_2} \int\limits_{a_1}^{a_2} f_{X_1 X_2}(u, v)\, du dv$$

for all values a_1, a_2, b_1, b_2.

NOTE:

$$\int\limits_{-\infty}^{a} \int\limits_{-\infty}^{\infty} f_{X_1 X_2}(u, v)\, dv du = F_{X_1 X_2}(a, \infty)$$

$$= F_{X_1}(a) = \int\limits_{-\infty}^{a} f_{X_1}(u)\, du$$

for every a, so that

$$\int\limits_{-\infty}^{\infty} f_{X_1 X_2}(u, v)\, dv = f_{X_1}(u).$$

Similarly $$\int\limits_{-\infty}^{\infty} f_{X_1 X_2}(u, v)\, du = f_{X_2}(v).$$

In general, if there are n random variables $X_1, \ldots, X_n$, Definition 2.18 is extended to

$$F_{X_1, \ldots, X_n}(a_1, \ldots, a_n) = P\{X_1 \leqslant a_1, \ldots, X_n \leqslant a_n\}.$$

If a joint density function exists

$$F_{X_1, \ldots, X_n}(a_1, \ldots, a_n) = \int\limits_{-\infty}^{a_n} \ldots \int\limits_{-\infty}^{a_1} f_{X_1, \ldots, X_n}(u_1, \ldots, u_n)\, du_1 \ldots du_n,$$

$$P\{a_1 < X_1 \leqslant a_1', \ldots, a_n < X_n \leqslant a_n'\}$$

$$= \int\limits_{a_n}^{a_n'} \ldots \int\limits_{a_1}^{a_1'} f_{X_1, \ldots, X_n}(u_1, \ldots, u_n)\, du_1 \ldots du_n,$$

and

$$\int\limits_{-\infty}^{\infty} f_{X_1, \ldots, X_n}(u_1, \ldots, u_n)\, du_n = f_{X_1, \ldots, X_{n-1}}(u_1, \ldots, u_{n-1}).$$

Often, one is interested in a random variable G which is a function of $X_1,..., X_n$. If a joint density function exists, the distribution of G can be obtained from the equation:

$$F_G(a) = P\{G \leqslant a\} = \int...\int_{R_a} f_{X_1,...,X_n}(u_1,...,u_n)\, du_1 \therefore du_n,$$

where R_a denotes the region in the n dimensional space of $u_1,..., u_n$ for which $G(u_1,...,u_n) \leqslant a$. If discrete, the analogous equation holds with integrals replaced by sums.

The expected value of G, computed by Definition 2.13, is given by

$$EG = \int_{-\infty}^{\infty} af_G(a)\, da,$$

where $$f_G(a) = F'_G(a).$$

If F_G is difficult to obtain, the expected value of G can also be computed by using the following, which is similar in form to Definition 2.14.

Definition 2.20:

$$EG = \begin{cases} \int_{-\infty}^{\infty}...\int_{-\infty}^{\infty} G(u_1,...,u_n)f_{X_1,...,X_n}(u_1,...,u_n)\, du_1... du_n \\ \sum_{\substack{\text{over all} \\ k_1,...,k_n}} G(k_1,...,k_n)P_{X_1,...,X_n}(k_1,...,k_n) \end{cases}$$

accordingly as there is a joint density or a probability function.

Example 2.29: An experiment consists of the production of a quantity of grade 5-D diesel fuel oil. X_1 and X_2, the random variables of interest, are values of the water and sediment content obtained via two different measurement techniques. Suppose it is known that the joint density function of X_1 and X_2 is

$$f_{X_1 X_2}: \quad f_{X_1 X_2}(u_1, u_2) = u_1 + u_2 \quad \text{if} \quad 0 \leqslant u_1 \leqslant 1(\%)$$
$$0 \leqslant u_2 \leqslant 1(\%)$$
$$= 0 \qquad \text{otherwise.}$$

Then

$$F_{X_1 X_2}: \quad F_{X_1 X_2}(a, b)$$
$$= \int_{-\infty}^{b} \int_{-\infty}^{a} f_{X_1 X_2}(u_1, u_2) \, du_1 \, du_2$$
$$= 0 \qquad\qquad (a < 0 \text{ or } b < 0)$$
$$= \int_{0}^{b} \int_{0}^{a} (u_1 + u_2) \, du_1 \, du_2$$
$$= \tfrac{1}{2}(a^2 b + b^2 a) \qquad (0 \leqslant a \leqslant 1, \, 0 \leqslant b \leqslant 1)$$
$$= \tfrac{1}{2}(b^2 + b) \qquad\quad (1 \leqslant a, \, 0 \leqslant b \leqslant 1)$$
$$= \tfrac{1}{2}(a^2 + a) \qquad\quad (0 \leqslant a \leqslant 1, \, 1 \leqslant b)$$
$$= 1 \qquad\qquad\quad (1 \leqslant a, b).$$

The density functions of X_1 and X_2 are:

$$f_{X_1}: f_{X_1}(u_1) = \int_{-\infty}^{\infty} f_{X_1 X_2}(u_1, u_2) \, du_2 = \int_{0}^{1} (u_1 + u_2) \, du_2 = \tfrac{1}{2} + u_1$$
$$\text{if } 0 \leqslant u_1 \leqslant 1$$
$$= 0 \qquad\qquad\qquad\qquad\qquad \text{otherwise,}$$

$$f_{X_2}: f_{X_2}(u_2) = \int_{-\infty}^{\infty} f_{X_1 X_2}(u_1, u_2) \, du_1 = \int_{0}^{1} (u_1 + u_2) \, du_1 = \tfrac{1}{2} + u_2$$
$$\text{if } 0 \leqslant u_2 \leqslant 1$$
$$= 0 \qquad\qquad\qquad\qquad\qquad \text{otherwise.}$$

A conservative laboratory might use only the larger of the two measurements; i.e. of interest is the new random variable $\quad G: \quad G(X_1, X_2) = \max(X_1, X_2).$

Then
$$F_G(a) = P\{\max(X_1, X_2) \leqslant a\}$$
$$= P\{X_1 \leqslant a, X_2 \leqslant a\}$$
$$= \int_{-\infty}^{a} \int_{-\infty}^{a} f_{X_1 X_2}(u_1, u_2) \, du_1 \, du_2,$$

F_G: $\quad F_G(a) = 0 \qquad\qquad\qquad\qquad\qquad (a < 0)$

$$= \int_0^a \int_0^a (u_1 + u_2) \, du_1 \, du_2 = a^3 \quad (0 < a < 1)$$

$$= 1 \qquad\qquad\qquad\qquad\qquad (1 \leqslant a),$$

and
$$f_G: \quad f_G(a) = 3a^2 \qquad\qquad (0 < a < 1)$$
$$= 0 \qquad\qquad\qquad (\text{otherwise}).$$

Hence $\quad EG = \int_{-\infty}^{\infty} a f_G(a) \, da = 3 \int_0^1 a^3 \, da = \tfrac{3}{4}.$

If it is computed by Definition 2.20,

$$EG = \int_{-\infty}^{\infty} \int_{-\infty}^{\infty} \max(u_1, u_2) f_{X_1 X_2}(u_1, u_2) \, du_1 \, du_2$$

$$= \int_0^1 \int_0^1 \max(u_1, u_2)(u_1 + u_2) \, du_1 \, du_2$$

$$= \int\int_{u_1 \geqslant u_2} u_1(u_1 + u_2) \, du_2 \, du_1 + \int\int_{u_2 \geqslant u_1} u_2(u_1 + u_2) \, du_1 \, du_2$$

$$= \int_0^1 \int_0^{u_1} u_1(u_1 + u_2) \, du_2 \, du_1 + \int_0^1 \int_0^{u_2} u_2(u_1 + u_2) \, du_1 \, du_2$$

$$= \int_0^1 \left(u_1^3 + \frac{u_1^3}{2}\right) du_1 + \int_0^1 \left(u_2^3 + \frac{u_2^3}{2}\right) du_2$$

$$= \tfrac{3}{4}.$$

A very important and useful property of expectations is

Theorem 3: If $c_1, ..., c_n$ are arbitrary constants and

$$G: \quad G(X_1, ..., X_n) = c_1 X_1 + ... + c_n X_n = \sum_{i=1}^{n} c_i X_i$$

then $\quad EG = c_1 EX_1 + ... + c_n EX_n = \sum_{i=1}^{n} c_i EX_i.$

A special case of the above, which will be of interest later, occurs when

$$EX_i = \mu, \qquad c_i = \frac{1}{n} \qquad (i = 1, ..., n).$$

Then $\qquad\qquad EG = \frac{1}{n} \sum_{i=1}^{n} EX_i = \mu.$

Definition 2.21: If $G: G(X_1, X_2) = (X_1 - EX_1)(X_2 - EX_2)$ then EG is called the *covariance* of the two random variables X_1 and X_2. This is usually denoted by $\text{Cov}(X_1, X_2)$. For the case of continuous random variables, the covariance may be computed according to

$$\text{Cov}(X_1, X_2) = \int_{-\infty}^{\infty} \int_{-\infty}^{\infty} (u - EX_1)(v - EX_2) f_{X_1 X_2}(u, v) \, du dv.$$

If X_1 and X_2 are discrete random variables, we obtain from the definition

$$\text{Cov}(X_1, X_2) = \sum_{\substack{\text{over all} \\ a, b}} (a - EX_1)(b - EX_2) P_{X_1 X_2}(a, b).$$

Theorems 1 and 3 can be used to obtain a form for $\text{Cov}(X_1, X_2)$ which is computationally convenient. This is

$$\text{Cov}(X_1, X_2) = E(X_1 X_2) - (EX_1)(EX_2).$$

Proof: By its definition

$\mathrm{Cov}(X_1, X_2)$

$\quad = E[(X_1 - EX_1)(X_2 - EX_2)]$

$\quad = E[X_1 X_2 - X_1(EX_2) - X_2(EX_1) + (EX_1)(EX_2)]$

$\quad = E(X_1 X_2) - (EX_1)(EX_2) - (EX_2)(EX_1) + (EX_1)(EX_2)$

$\quad = E(X_1 X_2) - (EX_1)(EX_2).$

Similarly, it can be shown that

$$\mathrm{Var}\, X = E(X^2) - (EX)^2.$$

Definition 2.22: The correlation coefficient between two random variables X_1 and X_2 is defined by

$$\rho_{X_1 X_2} = \frac{\mathrm{Cov}(X_1, X_2)}{\sigma_{X_1}\sigma_{X_2}}.$$

NOTE:† (a) $-1 \leqslant \rho \leqslant 1$.

(b) If there is a linear relationship between two random variables, i.e. one of the form

$$X_1 = \alpha + \beta X_2 \quad \text{for any } \alpha, \beta,$$

then, the correlation coefficient,

$$\rho_{X_1 X_2} = \begin{cases} 1 & \text{if } \beta > 0 \\ -1 & \text{if } \beta < 0 \end{cases}.$$

The converse of the above is also true. That is, if the correlation coefficient between two random variables is 1 or -1, then a linear relationship exists between the random variables ($\beta > 0$ if $\rho_{X_1 X_2} = 1$, $\beta < 0$ if $\rho_{X_1 X_2} = -1$).

Example 2.30: As a computational illustration, the covariance between the two random variables, $T =$ tensile

† For a proof of these properties of the correlation coefficient, see Feller, p. 222.

strength and Y = yield point, of Example 2.28 will be obtained.

It is easily verified that ET = 48,125 psi and that EY = 17,500 psi. Then, by Definition 2.22:

$$\text{Cov}(T, Y) = E[(T-ET)(Y-EY)]$$

$$= (45,000-48,125)(15,000-17,500)\tfrac{1}{4}$$

$$+(50,000-48,125)(18,000-17,500)\tfrac{1}{2}$$

$$+(45,000-48,125)(18,000-17,500)\tfrac{1}{8}$$

$$+(50,000-48,125)(20,000-17,500)\tfrac{1}{8}$$

$$\sim 3{\cdot}2\times10^6.$$

Example 2.31: The covariance between the random variables X_1 and X_2 in Example 2.29 will be computed:

$$E(X_1 X_2) = \int_{-\infty}^{\infty} \int_{-\infty}^{\infty} ab(a+b)\,dadb$$

$$= \int_0^1 \int_0^1 (a^2b+ab^2)\,dadb = \tfrac{1}{3}.$$

$$E(X_1) = \int_{-\infty}^{\infty} \int_{-\infty}^{\infty} a(a+b)\,dadb$$

$$= \int_0^1 \int_0^1 (a^2+ab)\,dadb = \tfrac{7}{12}.$$

Similarly, $EX_2 = \tfrac{7}{12}$.

Consequently,

$$\text{Cov}(X_1 X_2) = E(X_1 X_2)-EX_1 EX_2$$

$$= \tfrac{1}{3}-\tfrac{7}{12}\cdot\tfrac{7}{12} = -\tfrac{1}{144}.$$

Theorem 4: If c_i $(i = 1,...,n)$ are arbitrary constants and

$$G: \quad G(X_1,...,X_n) = \sum_{i=1}^{n} c_i X_i$$

then

$$\operatorname{Var} G = \sum_{i=1}^{n} c_i^2 \operatorname{Var} X_i + 2 \sum_{k=i+1}^{n} \sum_{i=1}^{n-1} c_i c_k \operatorname{Cov}(X_i, X_k).$$

Proof: By Definition 2.16

$$\operatorname{Var} G = \operatorname{Var}\Big(\sum_{i=1}^{n} c_i X_i\Big) = E\Big[\sum_{i=1}^{n} c_i X_i - E \sum_{i=1}^{n} c_i X_i\Big]^2$$

$$= E[\sum c_i X_i - \sum c_i E X_i]^2 = E[\sum c_i(X_i - E X_i)]^2$$

$$= E\Big[\sum c_i^2(X_i - E X_i)^2 +$$

$$+ 2 \sum_{k=i+1}^{n} \sum_{i=1}^{n-1} c_i c_k(X_i - E X_i)(X_k - E X_k)\Big].$$

The application of Theorem 3 yields

$$\sum_{i=1}^{n} c_i^2 E(X_i - E X_i)^2 + 2 \sum_{k=i+1}^{n} \sum_{i=1}^{n-1} c_i c_k E(X_i - E X_i)(X_k - E X_k)$$

which is equivalent to the desired result.

It is important to note that if

$$\operatorname{Cov}(X_i, X_k) = 0 \quad \text{for all} \quad i \neq k,$$

then $$\operatorname{Var} G = \sum_{i=1}^{n} c_i^2 \operatorname{Var} X_i.$$

EXERCISES—VII

1. If C_1 and C_2 are constants, X_1 and X_2 continuous random variables, and $G: \quad G(X_1, X_2) = C_1 X_1 + C_2 X_2,$

Prove: $EG = C_1 EX_1 + C_2 EX_2.$

2. An experiment gives rise to a sample space $\Omega = \{w_1, w_2, w_3\}$. It is known that the following probabilities may be associated with each outcome:

$$P\{w_1\} = \tfrac{1}{2}$$
$$P\{w_2\} = \tfrac{1}{4}$$
$$P\{w_3\} = \tfrac{1}{4}.$$

Two random variables X and Y are of interest which take on values as follows:

$$X: \quad X(w_1) = 1 \qquad\qquad Y: \quad Y(w_1) = 1$$
$$X(w_2) = 2 \qquad\qquad Y(w_2) = 2$$
$$X(w_3) = 3 \qquad\qquad Y(w_3) = 3.$$

(a) Describe F_{XY}.

(b) Compute ρ_{XY}.

(c) Compute $E(3X-4Y)$.

3. A textile processor grades his product as to color density and number of defects of a certain type per loom. There are five categories of color (denoted by $C_1,...,C_5$) and three categories of quality (Q_1, Q_2, Q_3).

It is known that the following probabilities can be associated with the event that a processed loom falls into a particular category combination:

Probabilities

	Q_1	Q_2	Q_3
C_1	0·24	0·12	0·04
C_2	0·12	0·06	0·02
C_3	0·12	0·06	0·02
C_4	0·06	0·03	0·01
C_5	0·06	0·03	0·01

The following matrix may be used to define a random variable of interest, dye costs (denoted by C) where the row refers to the appropriate color category and the column identifies the quality characteristic.

Dye costs

	Q_1	Q_2	Q_3
C_1	1·50	0·75	0·50
C_2	1·50	0·75	0·50
C_3	0·75	0·75	0·50
C_4	0·50	0·50	0·25
C_5	0·50	0·25	0·25

Similarly, the matrix given below indicates the values taken by another random variable of interest, distribution costs (denoted by S).

Distribution costs

	Q_1	Q_2	Q_3
C_1	0·10	0·10	0·50
C_2	0·10	0·10	0·50
C_3	0·10	0·10	0·50
C_4	0·25	0·25	0·50
C_5	0·25	0·25	0·50

(a) Describe F_{CS}, F_C, F_S.

(b) Compute: EC, ES.

(c) $\text{Cov}(C, S)$.

(d) ρ_{CS}.

(e) $E(C+S)$.

(f) σ_{C+S}.

(g) Use Chebyshev's inequality to give an upper bound to

$$P\{|(C+S) - E(C+S)| > 0·10\}.$$

4. A hosiery company wishes to decide how many pairs of hosiery to produce in each of the next two months. We denote the number of pairs of hosiery produced in each of the months respectively by b_1 and b_2. The random variables X_1 and X_2 are the demand for hosiery, in pairs, in the respective months. Suppose X_1 and X_2 have the following joint density function:

$f_{X_1 X_2}$: $f_{X_1 X_2}(a_1, a_2)$

$$= \begin{cases} k & \text{if } 2{,}000 \leqslant a_1 \leqslant 3{,}000 \text{ and } 1{,}000 \leqslant a_2 \leqslant 2{,}000 \\ 0 & \text{otherwise} \end{cases}.$$

(a) Find k. $= 10^{-6}$

(b) Describe $F_{X_1 X_2}$, F_{X_1}, F_{X_2}.

(c) Compute EX_1, EX_2, $E(X_1 + X_2)$.

(d) σ_{X_1}, σ_{X_2}, $\text{Cov}(X_1, X_2)$.

If $b_1 > X_1$, the resulting excess of first-month production $(b_1 - X_1)$ is carried forward as inventory to the beginning of the second month. Similarly, if $b_1 + b_2 > X_1 + X_2$, the excess $(b_2 + b_1 - X_1 - X_2)$ production is carried forth to the beginning of the third month.

The following costs are incurred in producing hosiery:

$0.45/pair—direct materials and labor in both months.

$0·05/pair—cost of carrying one pair in inventory for one month.

The selling price of hosiery is $0.75/pair in both months. Four assumptions will help to simplify the problem:

(1) There is no initial hosiery inventory.
(2) Production and demand occur simultaneously at the beginning of each month.
(3) Inventory remaining at the end of the second month cannot be sold.
(4) Unsatisfied demand in a month is merely lost business and cannot be satisfied by production in later months.
   (a) Describe the random variable which respresents the total profit from the production and sale of hosiery in a period of two months.
   (b) Set up the computational form for the expected total profit.

2.9. *Conditional probability*

In some experiments, usually as a result of some special interest, it is desired to consider only a portion of the sample space.

For example, if an experiment is to toss a coin twice, the sample space will contain four outcomes

$$\{(H, T), (H, H), (T, H), (T, T)\}.$$

One may consider the experiment after only half of it has been performed, i.e. the coin has been tossed only once and it is known that, say, heads was the result. Then, in reconsidering the sample space, it is only necessary to consider the event consisting of outcomes (H, T) and (H, H). Under these conditions the probabilities associated with these outcomes must be reassigned. This reassignment of probabilities to events in the sub-sample space can be accomplished in a natural fashion in accordance with the following scheme.

Definition 2.23: Let A and B denote events in some sample space (assume that $P\{A\} > 0$). Then the *conditional probability* of the event B *given* that the event A has occurred, denoted by $P\{B|A\}$, is defined as

$$P\{B|A\} = \frac{P(A \cap B)}{P(A)}.$$

The definition of $P\{B|A\}$ can be motivated by the frequency interpretation of probability discussed earlier. The ratio

$$\frac{n\{A \cap B\}}{n\{A\}}$$

denotes the proportion of times with which the event $A \cap B$ occurs in all those trials in which the event A occurs —a natural measure of the relative likelihood of the event $A \cap B$ compared to the likelihood of the event A. Dividing the numerator and the denominator by n, the total number of trials, and letting $n \to \infty$, we have

$$\lim_{n \to \infty} \left(\frac{n\{A \cap B\}}{n} \bigg/ \frac{n\{A\}}{n} \right) = \lim_{n \to \infty} \frac{n\{A \cap B\}}{n} \bigg/ \lim_{n \to \infty} \frac{n\{A\}}{n}$$
$$= \frac{P\{A \cap B\}}{P\{A\}}.$$

Example 2.32: The probabilities associated with the values taken by the two random variables of interest in Example 2.28 may be put in the following tabular form:

	$Y = 15{,}000$	$Y = 18{,}000$	$Y = 20{,}000$
$T = 45{,}000$	$\frac{1}{4}$	$\frac{1}{8}$	0
$T = 50{,}000$	0	$\frac{1}{2}$	$\frac{1}{8}$

Let A denote the event $\{T = 45{,}000\}$,
  B denote the event $\{Y = 18{,}000\}$.

Then

$$P\{B|A\} = \frac{P\{A \cap B\}}{P\{A\}} = \frac{P\{T = 45{,}000,\, Y = 18{,}000\}}{P\{T = 45{,}000\}}$$

$$= \frac{\frac{1}{8}}{\frac{1}{4} + \frac{1}{8}} = \tfrac{1}{3}.$$

Example 2.33: Let A denote the event $\{\tfrac{1}{2} < X_1 \leqslant 1\}$,
  B denote the event $\{\tfrac{1}{2} < X_2 \leqslant 1\}$,

where X_1 and X_2 are the random variables of interest in Example 2.29. Then

$P\{A \cap B\}$

$$= F_{X_1 X_2}(1, 1) - F_{X_1 X_2}(\tfrac{1}{2}, 1) - F_{X_1 X_2}(1, \tfrac{1}{2}) + F_{X_1 X_2}(\tfrac{1}{2}, \tfrac{1}{2})$$

$$= 1 - \tfrac{3}{8} - \tfrac{3}{8} + \tfrac{1}{8} = \tfrac{3}{8}$$

and

$$P\{A\} = F_{X_1}(1) - F_{X_1}(\tfrac{1}{2})$$

$$= 1 - \int\limits_0^{\frac{1}{2}} (\tfrac{1}{2} + u_1)\, du_1 = \tfrac{5}{8}.$$

Hence, $$P\{B|A\} = \frac{\frac{3}{8}}{\frac{5}{8}} = \tfrac{3}{5}.$$

2.10. *Statistical independence*

Definition 2.24: Two events, A and B, are said to be *statistically independent* if

$$(1) \quad P\{A \cap B\} = P\{A\} \cdot P\{B\}.$$

When this holds and if $P\{A\} \cdot P\{B\} \neq 0$, it follows that

$$(2) \qquad P\{B|A\} = P\{B\}$$

and $$(3) \qquad P\{A|B\} = P\{A\},$$

i.e. the conditional probability of B given that the event

A has occurred (or that of A given that B has occurred) is the same as the original, or unconditional, probability of B (of A). Conversely, it can be seen that if (2) or (3) holds, then (1) is true.

A natural extension is

Definition 2.25: The n events $E_1,..., E_n$ are called *statistically independent* if

$$P\{E_i \cap E_j\} = P\{E_i\}P\{E_j\} \qquad \text{for all } i \neq j,$$

$$P\{E_i \cap E_j \cap E_k\} = P\{E_i\}P\{E_j\}P\{E_k\} \text{ for all } i \neq j \neq k,$$

$$\vdots \qquad\qquad\qquad \vdots$$

$$P\{E_1 \cap E_2 \cap ... \cap E_n\} = \prod_{i=1}^{n} P\{E_i\}.$$

Example 2.34: For the experiment in which a coin is tossed twice, if

$$P\{H, H\} = P\{H, T\} = P\{T, H\} = P\{T, T\} = \tfrac{1}{4}$$

and if A denotes the event H on first toss,

and B denotes the event T on second toss,

then $$P\{B|A\} = P\{B\} = \tfrac{1}{2}.$$

Hence, the two events are independent. Equivalently, they are independent since

$$P\{A \cap B\} = P\{H, T\} = \tfrac{1}{4}$$

and $$P\{A\} \cdot P\{B\} = \tfrac{1}{2} \cdot \tfrac{1}{2} = \tfrac{1}{4}.$$

The most important counterpart in the experimental world to the mathematical concept of statistical independence is the following:

An experiment is performed in n stages in such a way that the outcome of the experiment at any stage does not affect either the manner in which any subsequent stage of the experiment is conducted or any outcome associated with a subsequent stage. Each stage is then *physically independent* of the others.

If a set of events is defined in such a way that each event consists of outcomes the occurrences of which are determined by a different stage of the experiment, then the events so defined are physically independent. The notion of statistical independence is intended to reflect this physical independence in the mathematical formulation.

Example 2.35: An experiment is to toss a coin twice. The tosses are to be carried out in such a way that they are physically independent (interpreted mathematically by assuming statistical independence). Suppose the coin is such that the probability of heads is p.

Let

E_1 be the event H on 1st toss $= \{(H, H), (H, T)\}$,

E_2 be the event H on 2nd toss $= \{(H, H), (T, H)\}$,

E_3 be the event T on 1st toss $= \{(T, H), (T, T)\}$,

E_4 be the event T on 2nd toss $= \{(H, T), (T, T)\}$.

Then, since the pairs of events E_1, E_2; E_1, E_4; E_2, E_3; and E_3, E_4 are independent,

$$P\{H, H\} = P\{E_1 \cap E_2\} = P\{E_1\}P\{E_2\} = p^2,$$
$$P\{H, T\} = P\{E_1 \cap E_4\} = P\{E_1\}P\{E_4\} = p(1-p),$$
$$P\{T, H\} = P\{E_3 \cap E_2\} = P\{E_3\}P\{E_2\} = (1-p)p,$$
$$P\{T, T\} = P\{E_3 \cap E_4\} = P\{E_3\}P\{E_4\} = (1-p)^2.$$

EXERCISES—VIII

The government is willing to make three attempts to launch a special satellite. Once one attempted launching is successful, *no further* attempts will be made. Suppose each attempt is physically independent of preceding attempts and that the probability of a successful launching on any given attempt is 1/5.

Consider the above rules as an *experiment* performed by the government to launch a satellite.

(*a*) List all points in the sample space.

(*b*) Compute the probability associated with each outcome in Ω.

(*c*) What is the probability that three attempts will be made?

(*d*) What is the probability of a successful launching on the third attempt?

(*e*) Suppose that the cost of an attempt is $1,000,000. Compute the expected cost of the experiment.

(*f*) Given that the first test has failed, compute the expected cost of the experiment.

2.11. *The binomial distribution*

In the process of generalizing Example 2.35 the binomial distribution may be derived.

Suppose the experiment is that of tossing a coin n times. Assume that the coin is such that the probability of a head on any one toss is p and that the separate tosses are made in such a way that events which depend only on one particular toss are statistically independent of events which depend on any other toss (i.e. assuming the mathematical reflection of physical independence).

Consider the random variable $X =$ number of heads in the n tosses. In deriving the distribution of X, it is required to determine $P_X(k)$ for $k = 0, 1,..., n$.

One outcome which gives rise to $\{X = k\}$ is the outcome

$$\{\underbrace{H,...,H}_{k}, \underbrace{T,...,T}_{n-k}\} = E_1 \cap ... \cap E_k \cap E_{k+1}^* \cap ... \cap E_n^*$$

where E_i = the event heads on the ith toss and E_i^* = complement of E_i = tails on ith toss. As a result of the assumption of statistical independence

$$P(\underbrace{H,...,H}_{k},\ \underbrace{T,...,T}_{n-k}) = \underbrace{P\{E_1\}...P\{E_k\}}_{k}\ \underbrace{P\{E_{k+1}^*\}...P\{E_n^*\}}_{n-k}$$
$$= p^k(1-p)^{n-k}.$$

However, every outcome which has exactly k heads and $(n-k)$ tails will make $X = k$ and will have the same probability associated with it. Hence, $P_X(k)$ is simply the total number of such outcomes multiplied by $p^k(1-p)^{n-k}$.

The number of these outcomes is just the number of combinations of n things taken k at a time, which is $\binom{n}{k}$. Hence,

$$P_X(k) = \binom{n}{k}p^k(1-p)^{n-k} \quad \text{for } k = 0, 1,..., n.$$

Example 2.36 (*Sampling with replacement*†): A lot contains ten switches of which two are defective. An experiment consists of drawing three switches from the lot as follows:

One switch is drawn, inspected, and then returned to the lot. This is repeated three times. The drawing is conducted in such a way that each time it is accomplished every switch in the lot has the same probability of being selected. (NOTE: Each drawing is physically independent of the others.) It is desired to compute the probability that all three items drawn are defective.

Since the experiment, as described, consists of three independent trials and the probability of drawing a defective in each trial is the same, it follows that the ran-

† Sampling without replacement leads to the *hypergeometric* distribution.

dom variable X (number of defective items in the three drawings) has a binomial distribution with parameters $n = 3$ and $p = \frac{2}{10}$. Hence

$$P_X(3) = \frac{3!}{3!\,0!}\left(\frac{2}{10}\right)^3\left(\frac{8}{10}\right)^0 = 0{\cdot}008.$$

EXERCISES—IX

A machine-tool manufacturer wishes to decide how many repairmen (r) to hire at \$10/day to service four special-purpose machines. Since the plant is operated during the day, the repairmen do their work on the night shift. Each repairman can repair one machine per shift. Thus, if the number of machine failures a day (N) is such that $N > r$, then the surplus (S) are repaired during the night shift by an outside contractor at \$20/machine repaired. Assume that the probability that any machine fails during a day is $0{\cdot}10$. Also assume that the probability of a machine failing is independent of both its past history and of other machine failures. Note that r can take on only non-negative integer values.

    (a) What is the probability function of the random variable N?

    (b) Compute σ_N.

    (c) Describe the surplus (S) in terms of r and N.

    (d) What is ES?

    (e) Describe the total cost (C) as a function of N and r.

    (f) Find EC.

    (g) Find the value of r which minimizes EC.

    (h) Does the assumption that the probability of machine failure in a day is independent of past history seem reasonable? Why?

2.12. *Independent random variables*

If one considers independent events of the form $\{X_i \leqslant a_i\}$ for $i = 1,..., n$, then by Definition 2.25

$$P\Big\{\bigcap_{i=1}^{n} \{X_i \leqslant a_i\}\Big\} = \prod_{i=1}^{n} P\{X_i \leqslant a_i\}.$$

However, $\qquad P\{X_i \leqslant a_i\} = F_{X_i}(a_i)$

and $\qquad P\Big\{\bigcap_{i=1}^{n} \{X_i \leqslant a_i\}\Big\} = F_{X_1,...,X_n}(a_1,...,a_n).$

Hence, it is natural to formulate

Definition 2.26: Random variables X_i $(i = 1,...,n)$ are called *independent* if

$$F_{X_1,...,X_n}(a_1,...,a_n) = F_{X_1}(a_1) \cdot F_{X_2}(a_2) \cdot ... \cdot F_{X_n}(a_n)$$

for *all* possible choices of $a_1,..., a_n$.

If a joint density function exists, this implies that:

$$f_{X_1,...,X_n}(a_1,...,a_n) = f_{X_1}(a_1) \cdot f_{X_2}(a_2) \cdot ... \cdot f_{X_n}(a_n)$$

and conversely. That is, the joint distribution function (or joint density function) of independent random variables must be factorable into the individual distribution functions (or density functions).

Example 2.37: An experiment consists of producing a photoflash bulb. Two characteristics of such bulbs when fired are: the brightness in candles per square inch of radiating surface (denoted by B), and the time to extinction (denoted by T).

Assume that the joint density function of the random variables is

$$f_{BT}: \quad f_{BT}(b,t) = e^{-(b+t)} \qquad \text{for} \quad b,t \geqslant 0$$
$$= 0 \qquad \qquad \text{otherwise.}$$

Then
$$f_{BT}(b,t) = f_B(b)f_T(t) \quad \text{for all possible values of } b \text{ and } t$$

where
$$f_B(b) = e^{-b} \qquad \text{if} \quad b \geqslant 0$$
$$= 0 \qquad \text{otherwise}$$

and
$$f_T(t) = e^{-t} \qquad \text{if} \quad t \geqslant 0$$
$$= 0 \qquad \text{otherwise.}$$

Hence, B and T are independent random variables.

Notice that the independence, in this case, of the random variables B and T does not reflect the notion of physical independence, since the experiment consists of only one stage (only one bulb is produced). This emphasizes the point that independence of random variables is a property of their joint distribution function. However, statistical independence, in most cases, is intended to reflect physical independence. For example, suppose that an experiment consists of producing two photoflash bulbs. Let B_1 denote the brightness of the first bulb and B_2 the brightness of the second. Assume that the production process is such that the brightness of one bulb has no effect on the brightness of the other. Then, because of the assumption of physical independence, we postulate that B_1 and B_2 are independent. Hence,

$$f_{B_1B_2}(t_1, t_2) = f_{B_1}(t_1)f_{B_2}(t_2) \qquad \text{for all } t_1, t_2.$$

Theorem 5: If X and Y are independent random variables, then the following properties hold:

(1) $E(XY) = EX \cdot EY$.

(2) $\text{Cov}(XY) = 0$.

(3) $\rho_{XY} = 0$.

(4) $\text{Var}(c_1 X + c_1 Y) = c_1^2 \text{Var} X + c_2^2 \text{Var} Y$.

Proof: Only property (1) will be verified and this only for the case in which a joint density function exists. Property (2) follows from (1); (3) and (4) follow from (2).

$$E(XY) = \int\limits_{-\infty}^{\infty} \int\limits_{-\infty}^{\infty} ab f_{XY}(a,b) \, da db.$$

Since X and Y are independent, f_{XY} may be factored, yielding

$$E(XY) = \int\limits_{-\infty}^{\infty} \int\limits_{-\infty}^{\infty} ab f_X(a) f_Y(b) \, da \, db$$

$$= \int\limits_{-\infty}^{\infty} a f_X(a) \, da \int\limits_{-\infty}^{\infty} b f_Y(b) \, db$$

$$= EX \cdot EY.$$

As an application of Theorems 3, 4, and 5, the expected value and the variance of a random variable having a binomial distribution may now be computed by viewing this random variable as the sum of independent random variables each having the same binomial distribution.

In the coin-tossing experiment last discussed, let

$X_i = 1$ if heads occurs on the ith toss,

$= 0$ if tails occurs on the ith toss

$(i = 1,...,n).$

Then, it was previously shown that the random variable $Y = \sum\limits_{i=1}^{n} X_i$ has a binomial distribution with parameters n and p. Now,

$$EX_i = 0P_{X_i}(0) + 1P_{X_i}(1)$$
$$= 0(1-p) + 1(p) = p.$$

Hence,

$$EY = E\sum_{i=1}^{n} X_i = \sum_{i=1}^{n} EX_i = \sum_{i=1}^{n} p = np.$$

Since the random variables X_i $(i = 1,...,n)$ are independent, it follows from the repeated application of Theorem 5 that $\text{Cov}(X_i, X_j) = 0$ if $i \neq j$. Therefore,

$$\text{Var}\, Y = \text{Var} \sum_{i=1}^{n} X_i = \sum_{i=1}^{n} \text{Var}\, X_i.$$

However,

$$\operatorname{Var} X_i = (0-p)^2 P_{X_i}(0) + (1-p)^2 P_{X_i}(1)$$
$$= p^2(1-p) + (1-p)^2 p = p(1-p).$$

Hence, $\quad \operatorname{Var} Y = \sum_{i=1}^{n} p(1-p) = np(1-p).$

2.13. *The law of large numbers*

If a fair coin is tossed repeatedly and the proportion of heads to the total number of tosses is recorded, it is intuitively expected that this proportion will tend toward $\frac{1}{2}$ as the number of tosses gets large. A theorem reflecting this 'law of averages' and called the *law of large numbers* follows.

Theorem 6: If $X_1, ..., X_n$ are independent random variables with

(1) $\quad EX_i = \mu,$

(2) $\quad \operatorname{Var} X_i = \sigma^2 \quad \text{for} \quad i = 1, ..., n$

and if another random variable is defined by

$$\bar{X}: \quad \bar{X}(X_1, ..., X_n) = \frac{1}{n} \sum_{i=1}^{n} X_i$$

then, for any constant $\delta > 0$

$$\lim_{n \to \infty} P\{|\bar{X} - \mu| > \delta\} = 0.$$

That is, the probability of as much as some arbitrarily small difference, δ, existing between $\bar{X}$ and μ approaches zero with increasing n. Alternatively, when n is very large, the probability is very close to one that the random variable $\bar{X}$ is very close to μ (its expectation, since $E\bar{X} = \mu$). This theorem emphasizes the importance of the expected value of a random variable in terms of the frequency interpretation of probability.

Before proving the theorem we note that in addition to

$$E\bar{X} = \mu$$

we also have $\quad \operatorname{Var}\bar{X} = \sigma^2/n.$

Proof: By Chebyshev's inequality

$$P\{|\bar{X} - E\bar{X}| > \delta\} \leqslant \frac{\operatorname{Var}\bar{X}}{\delta^2}$$

i.e. $\qquad P\{|\bar{X} - \mu| > \delta\} \leqslant \frac{\sigma^2}{n\delta^2}.$

Hence, $\qquad \lim_{n \to \infty} P\{|\bar{X} - \mu| > \delta\} = 0.$

This law of large numbers provides a theoretical counterpart of the frequency interpretation of probability given earlier. In this vein, consider the case in which the n random variables are

$X_i: \quad X_i = 1 \quad$ if an event E of interest occurs on the ith trial,

$\qquad\quad = 0 \quad$ if an event E of interest does not occur on the ith trial,

and

$$P_{X_i}(1) = p \qquad (i = 1,...,n)$$

$$P_{X_i}(0) = 1 - p.$$

Then $\qquad \bar{X} = \dfrac{n\{E\}}{n}, \qquad E\bar{X} = p$

and by the law of large numbers, for any $\delta > 0$

$$\lim_{n \to \infty} P\{|\bar{X} - p| > \delta\} = 0,$$

i.e. the probability is close to 1 that the difference between the relative frequency ($\bar{X} = n\{E\}/n$) of the occurrence of an event E and the probability of this event $P\{E\}$ will be very small, for sufficiently large n.

It should be noted, however, that this theorem *does not imply*, even in a probability sense, that, for large n, the actual number of occurrences of the event is close to the expected number of occurrences of the event. The statement is valid only for *relative* frequencies. To make this point, suppose the actual number of occurrences is $\frac{1}{2}n + \log n$. As $n \to \infty$ this deviates from $\frac{1}{2}n$ by $\log n$—a large number. However, the relative frequency

$$\frac{\frac{1}{2}n + \log n}{n} \to \frac{1}{2} \quad \text{as} \quad n \to \infty.$$

EXERCISES—X

1. Prove that properties (2) and (4) of Theorem 5 hold.

2. If $X_1,..., X_n$ are the independent random variables defined on p. 77 and if

$$G: \quad G(X_1,...,X_n) = \frac{1}{n}\sum_{i=1}^{n} X_i$$

show that $$EG = p,$$

$$\text{Var } G = \frac{p(1-p)}{n}.$$

3. If $X_1,..., X_n$ are independent random variables each having the same expected value μ and variance σ^2 show that

(a) $E\bar{X} = \mu$;

(b) $\text{Var } \bar{X} = \sigma^2/n$.

If $G(X_1,...,X_n) = (\bar{X} - \mu)/\sigma_{\bar{X}}$, show that

(c) $EG = 0$;

(d) $\sigma_G = 1$.

4. Suppose that a plant consists of two separate production lines each of which feed the same product into a stockpile. An experiment consists of observing the behavior of the stockpile at the end of a day in which both lines were operating. Assume that X and Y, the random variables describing the output from each line, are independent, each with probability function given below:

$$P_X(0) = P_Y(0) = \tfrac{1}{3},$$

$$P_X(6) = P_Y(6) = \tfrac{2}{3}.$$

Let G_1 be the random variable denoting the condition of the stockpile after one day's production and G_2 the random variable describing the condition of the stockpile after two days' production.

(a) Give the probability function of G_1.

(b) Give the probability function of G_2.

(c) Compute EG_1, EG_2, σ_{G_1}, σ_{G_2}.

5. A production line consists of two work stations in a series arrangement. Let X be a random variable denoting the production rate (in units per day) of one station and Y a random variable describing the production rate at the other station. The resulting production rate of the line is controlled by the lower of the two in any particular day. Assume that the experiment is to run the line for one day, and let G_1 be a random variable describing the output of the line, i.e. $G_1(X, Y) = \min(X, Y)$.

Suppose that the probability functions of X and Y are the same as in problem 4 above.

(a) Give the probability function of G_1.

(b) Compute EG_1, σ_{G_1}.

Let G_2 be the random variable describing the behavior of the inventory (assuming no withdrawals) after two days' production.

(c) Give the probability function of G_2.

(d) Compute EG_2, σ_{G_2}.

6. A production situation consists of one machine (A) feeding material into a bank at the end of one hour's production and another machine (B) demanding material from the bank at the

start of the next hour's production. Let X be the random variable describing the output of machine A and Y the random variable describing the demand of machine B. Assume that the probability functions for X and Y are as given in problem 4 above.

Let G_1 denote the condition of the stockpile after one hour's production and G_2 the stockpile condition after two hours' production.

   (a) Give the probability function of G_1 and of G_2.
   (b) Compute the expected values and the variances of G_1 and G_2.

7. The lag in weeks between ordering and delivering of a product is usually called 'lead time.' A company has found that its 'lead time' (L) in weeks is the sum of two independent components: delay due to 'paperwork' (X) and delay due to 'production' (Y). Suppose X and Y have the following density functions:

$$f_X: \quad f_X(a) = \begin{cases} 1 & \text{if } 0 \leqslant a \leqslant 1 \\ 0 & \text{otherwise} \end{cases}$$

$$f_Y: \quad f_Y(b) = \begin{cases} 1 & \text{if } 0 \leqslant b \leqslant 1 \\ 0 & \text{otherwise} \end{cases}.$$

Give the cumulative distribution function of L.

8. Suppose that X_1 and X_2 are independent random variables each having a Poisson distribution with parameters, respectively, λ_1 and λ_2. Show that the random variable

$$G: \quad G(X_1, X_2) = X_1 + X_2$$

has a Poisson distribution with parameter equal to $\lambda_1 + \lambda_2$.

9. A table manufacturer uses a process which has the property that the length of the sides are independent normally distributed random variables, each with mean equal to 30 inches and standard deviation equal to 1 inch. If one table is produced, compute

   (a) the probability that the perimeter of the table is less than 122 inches;
   (b) the expected area of the top (assume that opposite sides are equal);
   (c) the variance of the area.

2.14. *The central limit theorem*

Occasions arise when it is of interest to know the probability associated with events of the form

$$E = \left\{ c \leqslant \sum_{i=1}^{n} X_i \leqslant d \right\}.$$

For example, a shaft might be constructed by fitting, end to end, n different sections. Suppose that X_i $(i = 1,...,n)$ denotes the length of the ith section. Then $\sum_{i=1}^{n} X_i$ represents the length of the assembled shaft. If there are specifications for the completed unit, it will be of interest to know approximately the proportion of shafts which meet specifications when assembled.

If c and d denote respectively the lower and upper specification limits and if X_i $(i = 1,...,n)$ are continuous random variables, then the probability that an assembled shaft is satisfactory is

$$P\left\{ c \leqslant \sum_{i=1}^{n} X_i \leqslant d \right\} = \int_{R} ... \int f_{X_1...X_n}(t_1 ... t_n) \, dt_1 ... dt_n$$

where R denotes the region in the n-dimensional space satisfying the conditions that $c \leqslant \sum_{i=1}^{n} t_i \leqslant d$.

For some circumstances the following theorem is applicable:

Theorem 7: If $X_1,...,X_n$ are independent random variables, each *normally* distributed with respective parameters (μ_i, σ_i^2), then, the random variable

$$G: \quad G(X_1,...,X_n) = \sum_{i=1}^{n} X_i$$

is *normally* distributed with parameters

$$\mu = \sum_{i=1}^{n} \mu_i, \qquad \sigma^2 = \sum_{i=1}^{n} \sigma_i^2,$$

i.e. $$P\left\{ a \leqslant \frac{\sum\limits_{i=1}^{n} X_i - \sum\limits_{i=1}^{n} \mu_i}{\sqrt{\left(\sum\limits_{i=1}^{n} \sigma_i^2\right)}} \leqslant b \right\} = \frac{1}{\sqrt{(2\pi)}} \int_a^b e^{-\frac{1}{2}t^2}\, dt.$$

Example 2.38: Suppose the shaft consists of three sections, X_1, X_2, and X_3, which have normal distributions with $\mu_1 = 5$, $\sigma_1 = 0\cdot1$, $\mu_2 = 8$, $\sigma_2 = 0\cdot2$, $\mu_3 = 10$, and $\sigma_3 = 0\cdot2$.

Specifications on the total length are $23\cdot0 \pm 0\cdot6$. The probability of meeting specifications is

$$P\left\{22\cdot4 \leqslant \sum_{i=1}^{3} X_i \leqslant 23\cdot6\right\} = P\left\{-2 \leqslant \frac{\sum\limits_{i=1}^{3} X_i - 23}{0\cdot3} \leqslant 2\right\}$$

$$= \frac{1}{\sqrt{(2\pi)}} \int_{-2}^{2} e^{-\frac{1}{2}t^2}\, dt = 0\cdot956.$$

In situations other than those in which the random variables are normal, the exact computation of this probability, i.e. the evaluation of the multiple integral given earlier, may be quite difficult.

For some of these cases, the central-limit theorem, given below, provides a means of approximating the multiple integral.

Theorem 8 (*Central Limit Theorem*): If $X_1,..., X_n$ are independent random variables each having the same distribution with

$$EX_i = \mu$$

and $$\mathrm{Var}\, X_i = \sigma^2 \qquad\qquad (i = 1,...,n)$$

then

$$\lim_{n \to \infty} P\left\{ a \leqslant \frac{\sum\limits_{i=1}^{n} X_i - n\mu}{\sigma\sqrt{n}} \leqslant b \right\}$$

$$= \lim_{n \to \infty} P\left\{ a\sigma\sqrt{n} + n\mu \leqslant \sum_{i=1}^{n} X_i \leqslant b\sigma\sqrt{n} + n\mu \right\}$$

$$= \frac{1}{\sqrt{(2\pi)}} \int_a^b e^{-\frac{1}{2}t^2}\, dt$$

analogous to the expression in Theorem 7.

Example 2.39: In the shaft assembly problem, if the random variables X_i satisfy the conditions of Theorem 8 and if $\sigma^2 = 1$, $\mu = \frac{1}{2}$, $n = 20$, and if the specification limits are 8 and 12, then $n\mu = 10$ and

$$P\left\{ 8 \leqslant \sum_{i=1}^{20} X_i \leqslant 12 \right\} = P\left\{ \frac{8-10}{\sqrt{20}} \leqslant \frac{\sum X_i - 10}{\sqrt{20}} \leqslant \frac{12-10}{\sqrt{20}} \right\}$$

$$\sim \int_{\frac{8-10}{\sqrt{20}}}^{\frac{12-10}{\sqrt{20}}} \frac{e^{-\frac{1}{2}t^2}}{\sqrt{(2\pi)}}\, dt = 0\cdot 34.$$

A more general version of the central limit theorem is also available which is applicable even when the random variables X_i do not have the same distribution.† Roughly speaking, this generalization holds for cases in which the contribution of each random variable in the sum is small relative to the total magnitude of the sum. For these

† See Feller, pp. 238–41.

cases $n\mu$ is replaced by

$$\sum_{i=1}^{n} EX_i = \sum_{i=1}^{n} \mu_i$$

and $\sigma\sqrt{n}$ is replaced by $\sqrt{\left(\sum_{i=1}^{n} \sigma_i^2\right)}$.

The role played by this general form of the central limit theorem is of major importance. It states that the sum of many independent random variables having arbitrary distributions tends to be normally distributed. This provides substantial motivation for the study of the normal distribution. More pertinent for engineering purposes, however, it supplies mathematical justification for the empirical evidence of the frequent appearance of approximately normally distributed random variables in engineering and scientific problems.

2.15. *Approximations*

2.15.1. BINOMIAL DISTRIBUTION APPROXIMATED BY THE NORMAL DISTRIBUTION

It has previously been shown that a random variable G which has a binomial distribution with parameters n and p could be derived as the sum of n independent binomially distributed random variables each with parameters $n = 1$ and p. Hence, since G meets the conditions of the central limit theorem with $EX_i = p$ and $\text{Var}\,X_i = p(1-p)$,

$$P\left\{a \leqslant \frac{G-np}{\sqrt{[np(1-p)]}} \leqslant b\right\} \to \frac{1}{\sqrt{(2\pi)}} \int_a^b e^{-\frac{1}{2}t^2}\, dt$$

as $n \to \infty$.

2.15.2. BINOMIAL DISTRIBUTION APPROXIMATED BY THE POISSON DISTRIBUTION

Suppose that a random variable Y which represents the number of traffic accidents on a turnpike during a fixed time period has a binomial distribution with parameters n and p. If n denotes the number of cars using the turnpike in this period, and if p, which denotes the probability of each car having an accident, is expressed as λ/n so that $EY = np = \lambda$, then

$$P_Y(k) = \binom{n}{k} p^k (1-p)^{n-k} \quad (k = 0, 1, ..., n)$$

$$= \binom{n}{k} \left(\frac{\lambda}{n}\right)^k \left(1 - \frac{\lambda}{n}\right)^{n-k}.$$

If $n \to \infty$ and λ is held constant, the above expression, in the limit, becomes

$$\frac{e^{-\lambda}\lambda^k}{k!} \qquad (k = 0, 1,...)$$

the Poisson probability function with parameter λ. Thus, for large n

$$P_Y(k) \to \frac{e^{-\lambda}\lambda^k}{k!}.$$

Hence, if a situation exists in which the probability of an event in a single trial is small but the number of trials is very large (λ/n is small for large n), then the random variable denoting the number of times that the event occurs has a binomial distribution which is very closely approximated by the Poisson distribution.

The above also provides justification for the study and application of the Poisson distribution in engineering problems. Situations occur quite often in which there are a large number of trials and in which the probability of an event occurring on any one individual trial is very small, e.g. traffic accidents, telephone calls arriving at switch-boards, and people arriving at a counter for service.

2.15.3. Poisson Distribution Approximated by the Normal Distribution

If G is a random variable having a Poisson distribution with parameter λ, then, it can be shown that

$$\lim_{\lambda \to \infty} P\left\{ a < \frac{G-\lambda}{\sqrt{\lambda}} \leqslant b \right\} = \frac{1}{\sqrt{(2\pi)}} \int_a^b e^{-\frac{1}{2}t^2} \, dt,$$

i.e. for large values of λ, the normal distribution with mean $= \lambda$ and variance $= \lambda$ can be used to approximate the distribution of G.

This approximation has been found satisfactory if $\lambda > 10$.

2.15.4. Correction for Continuity

For most engineering applications, the use of the normal distribution to approximate the probabilities associated with random variables which have either binomial or Poisson distributions in the form given in the preceding pages is satisfactory. It should be noted, however, that the foregoing procedure does not permit the direct computation of the probabilities associated with the event that these random variables take on particular values. This problem stems from the use of the distribution function of a continuous random variable to approximate that of a discrete random variable. In order to motivate a simple method for alleviating this difficulty, the geometrical aspects of the approximating procedure are discussed below. As an example, consider the portion of the line graph of a random variable, Y, having a Poisson distribution with parameter $\lambda = 15$ shown below in Figure 6.

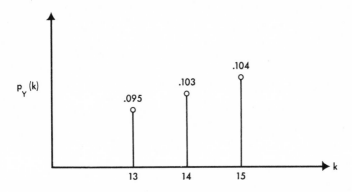

FIG. 6. Portion of the line graph of the probability function of a random variable having a Poisson distribution with $\lambda = 15$.

Since it is desired to approximate the heights of these lines by areas under a curve, the first step is to replace each of the lines by a rectangle equivalent in area to the height. This is accomplished, as shown in Figure 7, by constructing a rectangle with base equal to one and height equal to $P_Y(k)$, which is centered about $(Y = k)$. Such a representation is commonly called a *histogram*.

The final step is the approximation of the histogram by the area under the graph of the continuous normal density function. As can be seen in Figure 7, it is now quite natural

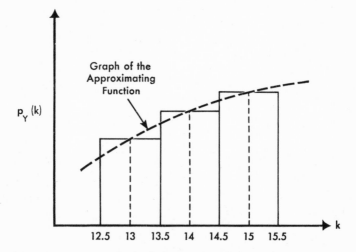

FIG. 7. Portion of the histogram of a random variable having a Poisson distribution with $\lambda = 15$.

to compute, as an example $P_Y(15)$, using correcting factors of $+\frac{1}{2}$ on the upper bound and $-\frac{1}{2}$ on the lower bound.

$$P\{Y = 15\} = P\{14{\cdot}5 < Y \leqslant 15{\cdot}5\}$$

$$= P\left\{\frac{14{\cdot}5 - 15}{\sqrt{15}} < \frac{Y - 15}{\sqrt{15}} \leqslant \frac{15{\cdot}5 - 15}{\sqrt{15}}\right\}$$

$$\sim \frac{1}{\sqrt{(2\pi)}} \int_{\frac{-0{\cdot}5}{\sqrt{15}}}^{\frac{0{\cdot}5}{\sqrt{15}}} e^{-\frac{1}{2}t^2}\, dt = 0{\cdot}103.$$

The same idea yields a slightly better approximation to

$$P\{a \leqslant Y \leqslant b\} \qquad \text{for} \quad a < b,$$

i.e. $P\{a \leqslant Y \leqslant b\} = P\{a - \frac{1}{2} \leqslant Y \leqslant b + \frac{1}{2}\}$

$$\sim \frac{1}{\sqrt{(2\pi)}} \int_{\frac{a - \frac{1}{2} - 15}{\sqrt{15}}}^{\frac{b + \frac{1}{2} - 15}{\sqrt{15}}} e^{-\frac{1}{2}t^2} \, dt.$$

EXERCISES—XI

1. A turbine shaft is made up of six different sections, the lengths of which are known to be independent, normally distributed random variables with expected values and variances, respectively:

(8·10, 0·05), (7·25, 0·04), (9·75, 0·06), (3·45, 0·04), (17·15, 0·10), (6·20, 0·07).

If the specifications call for the assembled shaft to be $52 \pm 1·5$ inches:

(a) What is the probability that an assembled shaft meets specifications?

(b) If ten shafts are assembled, compute exactly, using the normal approximation, and the Poisson approximation, the following probabilities:

    (1) at least nine shafts meet specifications;

    (2) less than nine shafts meet specifications;

    (3) exactly nine shafts meet specifications.

(c) Repeat part (b) where the new specifications are $52 \pm 0·5$ inches.

2. The number of lost-time accidents per week (N) in a large plant has been found to have a Poisson distribution with $\lambda = 8$.

(a) Compute, both exactly and using the normal approximation:

    (1) $P\{3 < N \leqslant 6\}$,

    (2) $P\{6 \leqslant N\}$,

    (3) $P\{N = 4\}$.

(b) Assume that the number of lost-time accidents in one week is independent of the number in preceding weeks and that the distribution does not change with time. Let N_3 denote the number of lost-time accidents over a three-week period.

Compute:

   (1) $P\{18 \leqslant N_3 \leqslant 19\}$,

   (2) $P\{20 \leqslant N_3 \leqslant 28\}$,

   (3) $P\{24 < N_3\}$,

   (4) $P\{N_3 = 24\}$.

NOTE: See problem 8 in Exercises X.

3. Suppose $X_1,..., X_{36}$ are independent and identically distributed random variables with $EX_i = 10$ and $\sigma^2_{X_i} = 4$ (for $i = 1, 2,..., 36$). Give an approximate numerical value to

$$P\left\{336 \leqslant \sum_{i=1}^{36} X_i \leqslant 372\right\}.$$

4. The density function of a random variable is

$$f_X\colon \quad f_X(a) = \begin{cases} \frac{1}{5} & \text{if } 0 \leqslant a \leqslant 5 \\ 0 & \text{otherwise} \end{cases}.$$

Suppose that $(X_1,..., X_{100})$ represents a sample of 100 independent observations.

   (a) Compute an approximate value to $P\{2\cdot4 \leqslant \bar{X} \leqslant 2\cdot6\}$.

   (b) If 400 independent observations are made, compute an approximate value to the probability of the same event.

   (c) Repeat (a) for two independent observations. Compare this with the exact answer. (See problem 7 of Exercises X.)

3

DECISION PROBLEMS

3.1. *Decisions with known distributions*

As previously discussed, if the distribution function of a random variable is known, then probabilities associated with various events of interest may be computed. Of equal importance is the application of this knowledge to the problems of decision making. An elementary illustration of this kind of application is the following:

Example 3.1: Using a standard process to manufacture a certain item, it has been found that the average profit per item is $0.75.

Let X denote the value of a critical characteristic of the item. Assume item specifications are such that

$$9 \leqslant X \leqslant 11.$$

Let the profit to the firm be denoted by the function

$$Z: \quad Z(X) = \$2.00 \quad \text{if} \quad 9 \leqslant X \leqslant 11$$
$$= -\$0.50 \quad \text{if} \quad |X-10| > 1.$$

A new proposed process is such that X will be normally distributed with mean $\mu = 10$ and variance $\sigma^2 = 1$.

The problem is to decide whether to use the proposed process for future manufacture or to continue with the old one.

A possible decision rule is as follows:

Adopt the new process if its $EZ > \$0.75$.

Continue with the old process if $EZ \leqslant \$0.75$.

Before proceeding with the example, a brief discussion will motivate this choice of a decision rule based on expected profit. The production of a series of items will generate a sequence of random variables $Z_1, Z_2,...,$ assumed to be independent and identically distributed, i.e. each random variable takes on the values \$2.00 or $-$\$0.50 according to whether an item produced meets or does not meet specifications. By the law of large numbers, it is known, in a probability sense, that the average profit

$$\left(\frac{1}{n}\sum_{i=1}^{n} Z_i\right)$$

approaches the expected profit (EZ) as the number of items produced (n) gets large. Thus, the firm can look forward to an average profit per item to be approximately equal to the expected profit. Hence, a decision rule in terms of the expected profit is reasonable.

The problem is continued. The probability function of Z is

$$P_Z: \quad P_Z(\$2.00) = \frac{1}{\sqrt{(2\pi)}} \int_{\frac{9-10}{1}}^{\frac{11-10}{1}} e^{-\frac{1}{2}t^2}\, dt = 0.683,$$

$$P_Z(-\$0.50) = 1 - P_Z(\$2.00) = 0.317.$$

The expected profit is

$$EZ = (2.00)(0.683) - (0.50)(0.317) = \$1.21.$$

Applying the decision rule, since $EZ > \$0.75$, the new process is adopted.

It should be pointed out that, in the above problem and discussion, there exists a tacit assumption that the number of items produced with the new process would be large so that the law of large numbers would provide an average profit per item equal to its expectation. Sometimes this assumption is inappropriate. For example, the introduction of the new process could introduce variation to the extent that a significant probability could exist of the production of a long enough sequence of defective items to bankrupt the firm before the law of large numbers had an opportunity to prevail. Under these circumstances, the probability of such an event should be computed, if possible, and taken into consideration.

3.2. *Decisions with unknown distributions*

If the distribution function of a random variable involved in a decision problem is unknown, it is usually necessary to resort to experimentation in order to gain information concerning the unknown distribution function. The data obtained from the experimentation are utilized in the form of an 'estimate' of the unknown distribution function. The 'estimate' may then be employed in a procedure similar to that in the preceding section.

The most common experimental procedure consists of a sequence of n identical (in so far as possible) independent stages which makes it possible to consider n independent random variables $(X_1,..., X_n)$ each presumably having the same (unknown) distribution function F_X.

Once the experiment has been performed and the random variables $(X_1,..., X_n)$ take on particular values, it is said that a *sample* has been obtained which consists of n independent *observations* on X.

One way to obtain an estimate of F_X is as follows:

For a particular value, b, first define the new random

variables

$$Z_i: \quad Z_i(X_i, b) = 1 \qquad \text{if } X_i \leqslant b$$
$$= 0 \qquad \text{otherwise}$$

for $i = 1,..., n$.

Then, another random variable

$$G: \quad G(Z_1,..., Z_n) = \frac{1}{n} \sum_{i=1}^{n} Z_i(X_i, b)$$

is equal to the proportion of X_i's such that $X_i \leqslant b$ $(i = 1,..., n)$.

It may be noted that

$$EG = \frac{1}{n} \sum_{i=1}^{n} EZ_i(X_i, b) = \frac{1}{n} \sum_{i=1}^{n} F_X(b) = F_X(b)$$

and by the law of large numbers

$$G \to EG = F_X(b) \quad \text{as} \quad n \to \infty$$

in a probability sense. Therefore, if n is large, the estimation procedure used above will yield a value approximately equal to $F_X(b)$.

3.3. *Estimation*

Often it is not necessary to estimate the entire function F_X. For decision-making purposes, it may be sufficient to estimate the value of some property of the distribution function, such as the expected value or the variance.

The general procedure used to obtain an estimate of a property, θ, is to form a function whose domain is the set of observations $(X_1,..., X_n)$ and whose range is the set of possible values of θ. A function of this type is called an *estimator* of the property θ. An estimator is, of course, a random variable with a distribution function which is dependent on the distribution function of the random variables $X_1,..., X_n$.

3.3.1. PROPERTIES OF GOOD ESTIMATORS

Since there are usually many possible functions which are capable of providing estimates, some means must be provided for the selection of a good estimator. Suppose that G is a random variable which has been proposed for use as an estimator of a property θ of a distribution function F_X. Then, in general, a very desirable characteristic for G would be to have its distribution highly concentrated about the value of θ, i.e. it is desirable that

$$P\{|G(X_1,..., X_n)-\theta| < c\} \quad \text{for any } c > 0$$

be as large as possible.

Some of the characteristics of good estimators which reflect the above general requirement are as follows:

Definition 3.1: A random variable G is said to be an *unbiased* estimator of a property θ, if $EG = \theta$.

Example 3.2: If

$$G: \quad G(X_1,..., X_n) = \frac{1}{n} \sum_{i=1}^{n} X_i$$

then it was previously shown† that $EG = EX$. Hence, G (usually denoted by $\bar{X}$) is an unbiased estimator of EX.

Example 3.3: If an unbiased estimate of $\operatorname{Var} X$ is required and if EX is known, then

$$G: \quad G(X_1,..., X_n) = \frac{1}{n} \sum_{i=1}^{n} (X_i-EX)^2$$

provides such an estimate.

† Theorem 3, p. 61.

Proof: Let $Y_i = (X_i - EX)^2$, then

$$EG = E\left(\frac{1}{n} \sum Y_i\right) = \frac{1}{n} \sum EY_i$$

$$= \frac{1}{n} \sum E(X_i - EX)^2 = \frac{1}{n} \sum \text{Var}\, X$$

$$= \text{Var}\, X.$$

Example 3.4: In the above, if EX is not known, then it can be shown that

$$G: \quad G(X_1,...,X_n) = \frac{1}{n-1} \sum_{i=1}^{n} (X_i - \bar{X})^2$$

is an unbiased estimator of $\text{Var}\, X$. (NOTE: G is usually denoted by s^2.)

A valuable property of unbiased estimators is that averages of different unbiased estimators of the same property are also unbiased. Hence, data can easily be combined.

Definition 3.2: A *consistent* estimator is one whose value approaches, in a probability sense, the value of the property of interest as the number of observations gets large.

Example 3.5: The random variable

$$\bar{X}: \quad \bar{X}(X_1,...,X_n) = \frac{1}{n} \sum_{i=1}^{n} X_i$$

is a consistent estimator of EX.

Proof:

The law of large numbers may be applied directly.

Example 3.6: As an example of an inconsistent, unbiased estimator of EX consider

$$G: \quad G(X_1,...,X_n) = \tfrac{1}{2}(X_1 + X_n).$$

G is unbiased since $EG = E[\frac{1}{2}(X_1 + X_n)] = EX$. However, the distribution of $\frac{1}{2}(X_1 + X_n)$ is the same for all n. Therefore, even as n increases, there is no approach in a probability sense of $G(X_1, ..., X_n)$ to EX.

Definition 3.3: A *minimum variance unbiased estimator* is one whose variance is least for all possible choices of unbiased estimators, or sometimes of all unbiased estimators within a certain group.

The variance can be viewed in most situations as a measure of precision of an estimator, i.e. usually the smaller the variance the better the chance of the estimator being near its expectation. It is therefore desirable to have an estimator with as small a variance as possible.

Example 3.7: An object is weighed on two different scales. Let X denote the weight recorded on the first scale and Y the value given by the second. If both scales are calibrated correctly, then $EX = EY = $ weight of object. However, the precision of the scales need not be the same, i.e.

$$\text{Var } X \neq \text{Var } Y.$$

Let the estimator of the weight of the object be

$$G: \quad G(X, Y) = bX + (1-b)Y \quad \text{where} \quad 0 < b < 1.$$

Note that $EG = $ weight of object. However, it is desirable to find that value of b which minimizes

$$\text{Var } G = b^2 \text{Var } X + (1-b)^2 \text{Var } Y.$$

It is easy to show that the above is minimized by setting

$$b = \frac{\text{Var } Y}{\text{Var } X + \text{Var } Y}.$$

Thus, if $\operatorname{Var} X = \operatorname{Var} Y$, the minimizing value is $\frac{1}{2}$ and a simple average of the two weights is required.

3.3.2. SPECIAL CASES OF INTEREST

Let $X_1,..., X_n$ be independent and identically distributed random variables whose distribution function is F_X.

(1) If F_X is normal, then the random variables $\bar{X}$ and s^2 are unbiased, consistent, minimum variance estimators of the parameters μ and σ^2 respectively.

(2) If F_X is Poisson, then $\bar{X}$ is an unbiased, consistent, minimum variance estimator of the parameter λ.

(3) If F_X is binomial with parameters $n = 1$ and p (i.e. $P_X(1) = p$, $P_X(0) = 1-p$) then $\bar{X}$ is an unbiased, consistent, minimum variance estimator of p.

EXERCISES—XII

1. Show that s^2 (see Example 3.4) is an unbiased estimator of $\operatorname{Var} X$.

2. If $X_1,..., X_n$ are independent, identically distributed random variables, show that

$$q^2: \quad q^2(X_1,...,X_n) = \frac{1}{2(n-1)} \sum_{i=1}^{n-1} (X_{i+1} - X_i)^2$$

is an unbiased estimator of $\operatorname{Var} X$.

(NOTE: q^2 is sometimes called the mean square successive difference.)

3. A large company has established a standard monthly cost by which it can compare the efficiency of operation of its three plants $(A, B, \text{and } C)$. The following deviations from the standard monthly cost in thousands of dollars were recorded at each plant for each of the last ten months as follows.

Give unbiased estimates of the variance and the expected value of monthly cost for each of the three plants, in terms of the standard cost for each plant.

A	B	C
11·56	−9·26	14·84
7·98	−11·36	−5.75
−10·94	−3·96	−7·78
−3·70	−5·16	−7·71
11·48	−12·30	−13·28
−22·16	9·10	13·14
11·28	11·20	−22·80
−7·16	28·50	−7·52
26·42	8·22	−14·99
−56·58	−28·12	2·48

NOTE: Compute the unbiased estimates of the variances using both s^2 and q^2.

4. Suppose that random variables X and Y have a joint cumulative distribution function $F_{XY}(a, b) = F_X(a)F_Y(b)$ (i.e. they are independent). Let $(X_1, Y_1),...,(X_n, Y_n)$ be a sample of n independent observations on the pair (X, Y).

It is of interest to obtain an estimate of EG where

$$G: \quad G(X, Y) = XY.$$

Two possible estimators are

$$G_1: \quad G_1[(X_1, Y_1),...,(X_n, Y_n)] = \bar{X}\bar{Y},$$

$$G_2: \quad G_2[(X_1, Y_1),...,(X_n, Y_n)] = \frac{1}{n}\sum_{i=1}^{n} X_i Y_i.$$

Show:

(a) $EG_1 = EG = EG_2$.

(b) $\operatorname{Var} G_1 \leqslant \operatorname{Var} G_2$.

3.4. *Decision rules*

Although the technique for decision making given in the preceding section, using an estimate of a distribution function, seems reasonable, objections can be raised from an engineering point of view.

The criteria which were suggested as aids for choosing estimators are not connected in a clear way with possible criteria of more direct interest to the decision maker.

The value associated with either a correct or an incorrect decision was not given quantative consideration in arriving at the criteria for use in the choice of an estimator. Nor was the cost of experimentation considered.

A more thorough approach to decision making is possible only through a complete examination of all facets of the problem which are pertinent both to the objectives and the risk-taking attitude of the decision maker.

A systematic way of implementing this approach is to evaluate all, or if not all, then all of a given group, of 'decision rules' in terms of the expected loss or gain to the decision maker; then, to choose the decision rule which minimizes this expected loss or maximizes the expected gain. By a *decision rule* we mean a rule which specifies

(1) the kind and amount of experimentation;

(2) the action which the decision maker is to take as a function of the results of the experiment.

By the loss, or gain, we mean the random variable related to the actual value which arises from the use of a given rule. Thus, associated with each rule there is an experiment, a sample space, a probability structure, and a random variable of interest which we call the loss or gain. The expected value of this random variable is the expression which will be used in the evaluation of each decision rule.

The direct effectiveness of a decision rule approach to

the solution of engineering problems will in many cases be limited. Very often, data concerning the pertinent facets of the problem are not available. Further, when all the data are available, the resulting mathematical problem involved in selecting a 'best' decision rule is usually of a very difficult nature; indeed, what is meant by 'best' may even become obscure. However, a valuable contribution of the decision-rule approach, even if it cannot always be carried through to its logical end, is that it can help the engineer focus on the problem of real concern and to formulate it in meaningful terms.

No attempt will be made to present a general theory of decision rules, although such a theory does exist. However, simple examples will be utilized to illustrate the spirit of such an approach.

Example 3.8: A manufacturer of rocket motors has two prototype motors of the same kind, both produced as far as is known in exactly the same way, available for shipment to a user with whom he has the following arrangement:

If a motor performs properly the manufacturer is paid $b. If the motor is defective, it causes a certain amount of damage for which the supplier is held responsible. Hence, the manufacturer compensates the user for this loss by an amount equal to $c.

Let the cost to produce a motor be $d and assume that the only available method of testing a motor involves destroying it. Further, assume that the cost of such a test is small relative to the cost of motor production and consequently may be neglected.

Listed below are some possible decision rules available to the supplier.

Rule I: Ship both motors.

Rule II: Select one motor at random† and test it. If it is defective, *do not* ship the remaining motor; if it is satisfactory, ship the remaining motor.

Rule III: Select one motor at random and ship it.

Rule IV: Select one motor at random and test it. If it is defective, ship the remaining motor. If it is satisfactory, *do not* ship the other motor.

Rule V: Select one motor at random and test it. Send the other motor.

Rule VI: Select one motor at random and test it. Keep the remaining motor.

It will be instructive to note the way in which the different experiments associated with each of the decision rules gives rise to different sample spaces. We shall evaluate only the first three rules.

Under Rule I the experiment is simply that of shipping two motors. Hence, the sample space consists of four outcomes. These are listed below together with their associated probabilities. It is convenient to identify the motors as A and B. Assume that the manufacturing process is such that the unknown probability of producing a defective motor is p.

$$\Omega_I = \begin{cases} \omega_1 = \text{both motors satisfactory} - P\{\omega_1\} = (1-p)^2 \\ \omega_2 = \text{only motor } A \text{ is defective} - P\{\omega_2\} = p(1-p) \\ \omega_3 = \text{only motor } B \text{ is defective} - P\{\omega_3\} = (1-p)p \\ \omega_4 = \text{both motors are defective} - P\{\omega_4\} = p^2. \end{cases}$$

† This should be interpreted as meaning that each motor has the same chance of being selected.

Let Z_I denote the monetary gain to the manufacturer when using Rule I. This quantity is a random variable defined as follows:

$$Z_I: \quad \begin{aligned} Z_I(\omega) &= 2(b-d) && \text{if } \omega_1 \text{ occurs} \\ &= b-c-2d && \text{if } \omega_2 \text{ or } \omega_3 \text{ occurs} \\ &= -2(c+d) && \text{if } \omega_4 \text{ occurs.} \end{aligned}$$

The expected gain, a function of p, is given by

$$\begin{aligned} EZ_I: \quad & EZ_I(p) \\ &= 2(b-d)(1-p)^2+(b-c-2d)2p(1-p)-2(c+d)p^2 \\ &= 2[(b-d)-p(b+c)]. \end{aligned}$$

Under Rule II, the experiment is to test one motor and then to either keep or ship the other motor according to whether the tested motor is defective or not. The sample space is

$$\Omega_{II} = \begin{cases} \omega_1 = \left\{ \begin{aligned} &A \text{ is tested and found defective} \\ &B \text{ is also defective and it is kept} \end{aligned} \right\} \\ \qquad\qquad\qquad\qquad\qquad P\{\omega_1\} = \tfrac{1}{2}p^2. \\[4pt] \omega_2 = \left\{ \begin{aligned} &A \text{ is tested and found defective} \\ &B \text{ is actually satisfactory but is kept} \end{aligned} \right\} \\ \qquad\qquad\qquad\qquad\qquad P\{\omega_2\} = \tfrac{1}{2}p(1-p). \\[4pt] \omega_3 = \left\{ \begin{aligned} &A \text{ is tested and found satisfactory} \\ &B \text{ is also satisfactory and it is shipped} \end{aligned} \right\} \\ \qquad\qquad\qquad\qquad\qquad P\{\omega_3\} = \tfrac{1}{2}(1-p)^2. \\[4pt] \omega_4 = \left\{ \begin{aligned} &A \text{ is tested and found satisfactory} \\ &B \text{ is defective, but it is shipped} \end{aligned} \right\} \\ \qquad\qquad\qquad\qquad\qquad P\{\omega_4\} = \tfrac{1}{2}(1-p)p. \\[4pt] \omega_5 = \left\{ \begin{aligned} &B \text{ is tested and found defective} \\ &A \text{ is also defective and it is kept} \end{aligned} \right\} \\ \qquad\qquad\qquad\qquad\qquad P\{\omega_5\} = \tfrac{1}{2}p^2. \end{cases}$$

$$\omega_6 = \begin{cases} B \text{ is tested and found defective} \\ A \text{ is actually satisfactory, but it is kept} \end{cases}$$
$$P\{\omega_6\} = \tfrac{1}{2}p(1-p).$$

$$\omega_7 = \begin{cases} B \text{ is tested and found satisfactory} \\ A \text{ is also satisfactory and it is shipped} \end{cases}$$
$$P\{\omega_7\} = \tfrac{1}{2}(1-p)^2.$$

$$\omega_8 = \begin{cases} B \text{ is tested and found satisfactory} \\ A \text{ is defective, but it is shipped} \end{cases}$$
$$P\{\omega_8\} = \tfrac{1}{2}(1-p)p.$$

If Z_{II} denotes the gain associated with utilizing Rule II, it is defined as

$$Z_{II}: \quad Z_{II}(\omega) = -2d \qquad \text{if } \omega_1, \omega_2, \omega_5, \text{ or } \omega_6 \text{ occurs}$$
$$= b-2d \qquad \text{if } \omega_3 \text{ or } \omega_7 \text{ occurs}$$
$$= -(2d+c) \quad \text{if } \omega_4 \text{ or } \omega_8 \text{ occurs}.$$

The expected gain is

$$EZ_{II}: \quad EZ_{II}(p)$$
$$= -2dp+(b-2d)(1-p)^2-(2d+c)p(1-p)$$
$$= (b-2d)-(c+2b)p+(b+c)p^2.$$

Under Rule III, the experiment is to select a motor and ship it. The sample space is

$$\Omega_{III} = \begin{cases} \omega_1 = \begin{cases} A \text{ is shipped} \\ \text{It is satisfactory} \end{cases} & P\{\omega_1\} = \tfrac{1}{2}(1-p). \\[2ex] \omega_2 = \begin{cases} A \text{ is shipped} \\ \text{It is defective} \end{cases} & P\{\omega_2\} = \tfrac{1}{2}p. \\[2ex] \omega_3 = \begin{cases} B \text{ is shipped} \\ \text{It is satisfactory} \end{cases} & P\{\omega_3\} = \tfrac{1}{2}(1-p). \\[2ex] \omega_4 = \begin{cases} B \text{ is shipped} \\ \text{It is defective} \end{cases} & P\{\omega_4\} = \tfrac{1}{2}p. \end{cases}$$

If Z_{III} denotes the gain associated with the use of Rule III, it is defined as follows:

$$Z_{III}: \quad Z_{III}(\omega) = b-2d \qquad \text{if } \omega_1 \text{ or } \omega_3 \text{ occurs}$$
$$= -(c+2d) \quad \text{if } \omega_2 \text{ or } \omega_4 \text{ occurs.}$$

The expected gain is

$$EZ_{III}: \quad EZ_{III}(p) = (b-2d)(1-p)-(c+2d)p$$
$$= (b-2d)-p(b+c).$$

The computation of the expected gain resulting from the use of the other three rules is left to the interested reader.

The evaluation of Rules I, II, and III for all values of p may be facilitated by drawing the graphs of the expected gain functions.

Suppose, for example, $b = 3$, $c = 1$, $d = 1$, then

$$EZ_I(p) = 4-8p$$
$$EZ_{II}(p) = 1-7p+4p^2$$
$$EZ_{III}(p) = 1-4p$$

(see Figure 8).

For any given value of p, it is possible to select the best of the three decision rules. This may be the case when there is a history of production such that a good estimate exists for the probability of a defective item being produced. For example, if $p = 1$, then EZ_{II} is greater than that associated with either Rule I or Rule III. Similarly, if $p = 0.5$, then Rule III leads to the largest expected gain. Further, if $p = 0$, then Rule I yields the best expected gain.

Unfortunately, however, none of these rules is consistently best for *all* possible values of p. This is the crux of the problem to be faced by the decision maker. It requires for its resolution some expression of the decision-maker's attitude toward the taking of risks. The problem allows the choice of just one decision rule. Somehow, the decision maker should choose a rule which will, in some

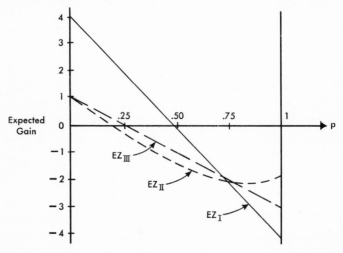

FIG. 8. The expected gain associated with decision Rules I, II, and III as a function of the probability, p, of producing a defective rocket motor (Example 3.8).

manner, utilize his experience and reflect his sense of values.

3.5. *Principles of choice*

3.5.1. BAYES'S PRINCIPLE

If the decision-maker's experience is such that his knowledge related to the pertinent parameter of the process can be expressed probabilistically, then this knowledge may be used in the following fashion.

In Example 3.8, assume that p is not a constant but actually varies from one time to another. However, suppose the variation is predictable enough such that p can be considered as a random variable with a density function f_p.

Define random variables as follows:

$$R_i: \quad R_i(p) = EZ_i(p) \quad (i = \text{I, II, III}; \\ 0 \leqslant p \leqslant 1),$$

i.e. $R_i(p)$ denotes the expected gain resulting from the use of decision Rule i for any value of p. Since R_i is a function of the (now considered) random variable p, it also is a random variable; it is of interest to consider its expectation, which is given by

$$ER_i = \int\limits_{-\infty}^{\infty} R_i(t) f_p(t)\, dt \quad (i = \text{I, II, III}).$$

It may be used to compare and choose among the decision rules. To illustrate this approach, assume that in Example 3.8 the density function of p has the form

$$f_p: \quad f_p(t) = 4 \qquad (\tfrac{1}{4} \leqslant t \leqslant \tfrac{1}{2}) \\ = 0 \qquad \text{otherwise.}$$

Then

$$ER_\text{I}(p) = 4 \int\limits_{\frac{1}{4}}^{\frac{1}{2}} (4-8t)\, dt = 1$$

$$ER_\text{II}(p) = 4 \int\limits_{\frac{1}{4}}^{\frac{1}{2}} (1-7t+4t^2)\, dt = -\tfrac{25}{24}$$

$$ER_\text{III}(p) = 4 \int\limits_{\frac{1}{4}}^{\frac{1}{2}} (1-4t)\, dt = -\tfrac{1}{2}.$$

Thus, it follows that Rule I is the best choice of the three.

The above kind of approach, considering the parameter of interest itself to be a random variable, is called a *Bayes approach*. A deficiency of this approach is that in most cases it is more realistic to view the parameter as an *unknown* constant. Consequently, it cannot be assumed to vary according to some *known* probabilistic law.

3.5.2. THE MINIMAX PRINCIPLE

Now suppose that there is no *a priori* information available, so that the Bayes approach is not feasible. Under these circumstances of complete uncertainty the decision maker has access to choice principles which can directly reflect the value system under which he operates. One such principle, which reflects an ultra-conservative point of view, is called the *minimax principle*. For a given rule, the expected gain is a function of the parameter of interest. This function will have a smallest value. The minimax principle says to choose that rule for which this smallest possible value is maximized.

Again, using Example 3.8 and Figure 6 it can be seen that the minimum expected gain under each of the rules is as follows:

Rule I: $\min[EZ_{\mathrm{I}}(p)] = EZ_{\mathrm{I}}(1) = -4,$

Rule II: $\min[EZ_{\mathrm{II}}(p)] = EZ_{\mathrm{II}}(\tfrac{7}{8}) = -\tfrac{33}{16},$

Rule III: $\min[EZ_{\mathrm{III}}(p)] = EZ_{\mathrm{III}}(1) = -3.$

Hence, Rule II is the best of the three rules in the minimax sense.

3.5.3. ADMISSIBILITY

The principle of admissibility can be used to limit the number of rules which need be considered. This arises when an expected gain function for one rule is greater, for *all* values of the parameter, than for some other rule. When this is the case, the latter rule is called *inadmissible* and need not be considered.

Although other choice criteria and principles are known, further discussion in those directions would go beyond the scope of our present interests. The notion of an evaluation of alternative decision rules on the basis of an examination of the graphs of the expected gain (or loss) functions, in terms of some suitable choice principle and, when possible, the use of information gained from experience with the process are the basic concepts stressed here.

To further illustrate this point of view, consider

Example 3.9: Suppose that the life (X) of an electron tube produced by a standard process is a random variable which is known to have an exponential distribution with parameter θ. (NOTE: $EX = 1/\theta$.)

Experience with this process has indicated that from time to time the value of the parameter θ may change. When such a change is believed to have occurred it is possible to adjust the equipment (at cost equal to \$1,000) so as to be sure that the next 1,000 tubes produced have lives whose distribution is characterized by the parameter $\theta = 1$.

The end item requirements for the tubes specify the scrapping of the item at a cost of \$10 to be borne by the tube supplier if the tube life X is less than 0·1 year. On the other hand if the tube lasts longer than 0·1 year the supplier receives a payment of \$5. One thousand tubes are required. The three decision rules given below are under consideration.

Rule I

One tube is to be produced and given an accelerated life test (which will be assumed to be completely reliable and to cost nothing). The result of this test is expressed as the life of the tube (X).

If $X \leqslant 0.3$ year the process is to be adjusted at a cost of \$1,000 so that $\theta = 1$. The 1,000 tubes are then produced.

If $X > 0.3$ year the 1,000 tubes are to be produced without further adjustments. (Assume that the process characteristics will remain stable for the 1,000-tube production.)

Rule II

Before any production, adjust the process, at cost equal to \$1,000, so that $\theta = 1$ and produce the 1,000 tubes.

Rule III

Produce the 1,000 tubes without any prior process adjustments. (Assume process stability for the 1,000 tube production run.)

We will evaluate these rules in turn.

The sample space associated with Rule I consists of two outcomes of interest, i.e. $\Omega = \{\omega_1, \omega_2\}$, where

$$\omega_1 = \begin{cases} (X \leqslant 0.3), \text{ the process is adjusted so that } \theta = 1, \\ \text{and the 1,000 tubes are produced. Each tube's} \\ \text{life has an exponential distribution with para-} \\ \text{meter } \theta = 1. \end{cases}$$

$$\omega_2 = \begin{cases} (X > 0.3), \text{ the process is not disturbed, and the} \\ \text{1,000 tubes are produced. Each tube's life has} \\ \text{an exponential distribution with unknown para-} \\ \text{meter } \theta. \end{cases}$$

The random variable of interest is the expected profit associated with each outcome in the sample space. If Z denotes this random variable, then it is defined as follows:

Z: $Z(\omega_1) =$ Expected profit if outcome ω_1 occurs,

$Z(\omega_2) =$ Expected profit if outcome ω_2 occurs.

After the values of Z are computed together with the probability function of Z, the expected value of Z may be determined. This value is the expected profit using Rule I.

$Z(\omega_1) =$ Expected income if the process is adjusted less the cost of adjustment.

Assuming that the process is adjusted, let the random variable Y denote the income to the tube supplier, from a single tube whose life is X. Hence,

$$Y: Y(X) = -\$10 \quad \text{if} \quad X \leqslant 0 \cdot 1$$
$$= \$5 \qquad \text{if} \quad X > 0 \cdot 1.$$

Then

$$EY = (-10)P\{X \leqslant 0 \cdot 1\} + (5)P\{X > 0 \cdot 1\}$$

where $\qquad P\{X \leqslant 0 \cdot 1\} = F_X(0 \cdot 1) = 1 - e^{-0 \cdot 1}$

and

$$P\{X > 0 \cdot 1\} = 1 - F_X(0 \cdot 1) = 1 - (1 - e^{-0 \cdot 1}) = e^{-0 \cdot 1}.$$

For the production of 1,000 tubes, the total expected income is

$$E \sum_{i=1}^{1,000} Y_i = \sum_{i=1}^{1,000} EY_i = 1,000 EY$$
$$= 1,000[(-10)(1 - e^{-0 \cdot 1}) + 5e^{-0 \cdot 1}]$$
$$= 1,000[15e^{-0 \cdot 1} - 10].$$

Hence, $\qquad Z(\omega_1) = \$3,573 - \$1,000 = \$2,573.$

The value of $Z(\omega_2)$ is obtained in a similar fashion, i.e.

$Z(\omega_2) = $ Expected profit if the process is not adjusted

$\qquad = 1,000[15e^{-0.1\theta}-10] = 15,000e^{-0.1\theta}-10,000.$

The required probabilities are

$$P\{\omega_1\} = P\{X \leqslant 0.1\} = 1-e^{-0.1\theta}$$
$$P\{\omega_2\} = P\{X > 0.1\} = e^{-0.1\theta}.$$

Then,

$$EZ = Z(\omega_1)P\{\omega_1\}+Z(\omega_2)P\{\omega_2\}$$
$$= Z(\omega_1)(1-P\{\omega_2\})+Z(\omega_2)P\{\omega_2\}$$
$$= Z(\omega_1)+[Z(\omega_2)-Z(\omega_1)]P\{\omega_2\}$$
$$= 2,573+[15,000e^{-0.1\theta}-10,000-2,573]e^{-0.1\theta}.$$

The evaluation of Rule II is facilitated by noting that since it involves adjustment of the process so that $\theta = 1$, the expected profit will be identical with $Z(\omega_1)$ associated with Rule I. Similarly, the expected profit associated with Rule III is given by $Z(\omega_2)$ associated with Rule I since in both cases no sampling is involved.

The graphs of the expected profit function for each of the decision rules are given in Figure 9.

Since, under all conditions of θ the expected profit under Rule I is never less than that under Rule III, the principle of inadmissibility may now be utilized to eliminate decision Rule III from further consideration.

If we assume the absence of any useful information about the values taken by the parameter θ and if the conservative minimax principle is employed, then an examination of Figure 9 indicates that Rule II is to be selected. That is, the minimum expected profit with Rule II is greater than the minimum expected profit with

Rule I; hence under a minimax policy, we would use Rule II.

On the other hand, suppose that the tube manufacturer has had considerable experience with the process and he believes that values greater than $\theta = 1\cdot8$ are extremely

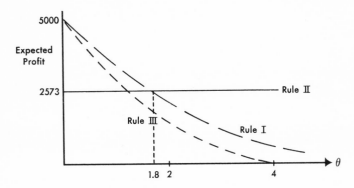

FIG. 9. The expected profit associated with each of the decision rules in Example 3.9, as a function of θ.

unlikely. If he could bear the losses if such eventualities occurred, he could then use Rule I and look forward (if his information is correct) to somewhat larger expected profits than those under Rule II.

The decision problem given below will serve to introduce a classical group of problems in statistical inference.

Example 3.10: Two production processes are used for a product. Although the processes are somewhat similar, some differences in their components tend to produce a difference in the quality of product. The process producing the better quality is the more costly. The quality of product is not directly observable; however, to some extent, a random variable X reflects the difference in the product. X is normally distributed with parameters given below.

Parameters	Process A	Process B
μ	20	22
σ	2	2

Suppose that an unidentified lot of 100 items, all of which are from one of the production processes is available. The terms of a proposed sale are as follows:

(1) If the lot is correctly described as from process B, a gain equal to $200 is made by the vendor for the items.

(2) If the lot is incorrectly described as from process B, the vendor gains nothing.

(3) If the lot is correctly described as from process A, a gain of $150 is made by the vendor.

(4) If the lot is erroneously described as from process A, the vendor gains $50 for the lot.

The cost of inspecting an item is $5.

The following decision rules have been proposed for the vendor's consideration:

Rule I: (a) Take a sample of four items from the lot.

          (b) Measure each of the items for dimension X. Compute $\bar{X}$.

          (c) If $\bar{X} > 21$ offer the lot as from B.

          (d) If $\bar{X} \leqslant 21$ offer the lot as from A.

Rule II: (a), (b) Same as Rule I.

          (c) If $\bar{X} > 20$ offer the lot as from B.

          (d) If $\bar{X} \leqslant 20$ offer the lot as from A.

Rule III: (a) Take a sample of nine items.

         (b), (c), and (d) Same as Rule I.

Rule IV: (a) Same as Rule III.

         (b), (c), and (d) Same as Rule II.

Before evaluating these decision rules, it will be instructive to consider briefly a basic property of rules of the type listed.

It has been previously established, by Theorem 7, that the random variable $\bar{X}$ will have a normal distribution with mean equal to μ and variance equal to σ^2/n. Hence, under Rule I, if the lot, and consequently the sample, was from process A then $E\bar{X} = 20$ and $\text{Var}\,\bar{X} = 4/4 = 1$. Therefore, the probability of concluding that process A produced the lot is given by

$$P\{\bar{X} \leqslant 21\} = \frac{1}{\sqrt{(2\pi)}} \int_{-\infty}^{\frac{21-20}{1}} e^{-\frac{1}{2}t^2}\,dt = 0\cdot841.$$

Thus, the probability of deciding (*correctly*) that the sample is from process A is greater than that of deciding (*incorrectly*) that it is from B.

On the other hand, if the sample was from a lot produced by process B, similar reasoning leads to

$$P\{\bar{X} \leqslant 21\} = \frac{1}{\sqrt{(2\pi)}} \int_{-\infty}^{\frac{21-22}{1}} e^{-\frac{1}{2}t^2}\,dt = 0\cdot159.$$

In this case, the probability of choosing (*correctly*) B as the source of the sample is greater than that of choosing (*incorrectly*) A.

This kind of obviously desirable property provides some motivation for choosing decision rules of the kind represented by the four given earlier.

Evaluation of Rule I: The random variable of interest will be taken to be the profit and will be denoted by G. Thus, first assume that the lot is from B, then

$$G_{\mathrm{I}}: \quad G_{\mathrm{I}}(\bar{X}) = \$200 - 4(\$5) = \$180 \quad \text{if} \quad \bar{X} > 21$$
$$= \$50 \ - 4(\$5) = \$30 \quad \text{if} \quad \bar{X} \leqslant 21.$$

The expected profit under these circumstances is

$$EG_{\mathrm{I}} = \$180 P\{\bar{X} > 21\} + \$30 P\{\bar{X} \leqslant 21\}$$
$$= \$180(0 \cdot 841) + \$30(0 \cdot 159) = \$156.$$

Similarly, if it is assumed that the lot is from A, we have

$$G_{\mathrm{I}}: \quad G_{\mathrm{I}}(\bar{X}) = \$150 - 4(\$5) = \$130 \quad \text{if} \quad \bar{X} \leqslant 21$$
$$= 0 - 4(\$5) = -\$20 \quad \text{if} \quad \bar{X} > 21.$$

Hence,

$$EG_{\mathrm{I}} = \$130 P\{\bar{X} \leqslant 21\} - \$20 P\{X > 21\}$$
$$= \$130(0 \cdot 841) - \$20(0 \cdot 159) = \$106.$$

Evaluation of Rule II: If the lot is from B

$$G_{\mathrm{II}}: \quad G_{\mathrm{II}}(\bar{X}) = \$200 - 4(\$5) = \$180 \quad \text{if} \quad \bar{X} > 20$$
$$= \$50 - 4(\$5) = \$30 \quad \text{if} \quad \bar{X} \leqslant 20.$$

Hence,

$$EG_{\mathrm{II}} = \$180 P\{\bar{X} > 20\} + \$30 P\{\bar{X} \leqslant 20\}$$
$$= \$180(0 \cdot 977) + \$30(0 \cdot 023) = \$177.$$

If the lot is from A

$$G_{\mathrm{II}}: \quad G_{\mathrm{II}}(\bar{X}) = \$150 - 4(\$5) = \$130 \quad \text{if} \quad \bar{X} \leqslant 20$$
$$= 0 - 4(\$5) = -\$20 \quad \text{if} \quad \bar{X} > 20.$$

Hence,

$$EG_{II} = \$130P\{\overline{X} \leqslant 20\} - \$20P\{\overline{X} > 20\}$$
$$= \$130(0\cdot5) - \$20(0\cdot5) = \$55.$$

Evaluation of Rule III: If the lot is from B

$$G_{III}: \quad G_{III}(\overline{X}) = 200 - 9(\$5) = \$155 \quad \text{if} \quad \overline{X} > 21$$
$$= 50 - 9(\$5) = \$5 \quad \text{if} \quad \overline{X} \leqslant 21.$$

Hence,

$$EG_{III} = \$155P\{\overline{X} > 21\} + \$5P\{\overline{X} \leqslant 21\}$$
$$= \$155(0\cdot933) + \$5(0\cdot067) = \$145.$$

If the lot is from A

$$G_{III}: \quad G_{III}(\overline{X}) = \$150 - \$9(5) = \$105 \quad \text{if} \quad \overline{X} \leqslant 21$$
$$= 0 - \$9(5) = -\$45 \quad \text{if} \quad \overline{X} > 21.$$

Hence,

$$EG_{III} = \$105P\{\overline{X} \leqslant 21\} - \$45P\{\overline{X} > 21\}$$
$$= \$105(0\cdot933) - \$45(0\cdot067) = \$94.$$

Evaluation of Rule IV: If the lot is from B

$$G_{IV}: \quad G_{IV}(\overline{X}) = \$155 \quad \text{if} \quad \overline{X} > 20$$
$$= \$5 \quad \text{if} \quad \overline{X} \leqslant 20.$$

Hence,

$$EG_{IV} = \$155P\{\overline{X} > 20\} + \$5P\{\overline{X} \leqslant 20\}$$
$$= \$155(0\cdot999) + \$5(0\cdot001) = \$155.$$

If the lot is from A

$$G_{IV}: \quad G_{IV}(\overline{X}) = \$105 \quad \text{if} \quad \overline{X} \leqslant 20$$
$$= \$-45 \quad \text{if} \quad \overline{X} > 20.$$

Hence,

$$EG_{IV} = \$105P\{\overline{X} \leqslant 20\} - \$45P\{\overline{X} > 20\}$$
$$= \$105(0\cdot5) - \$45(0\cdot5) = \$30.$$

A summary of the expected profits using each of the

decision rules, under the two possible conditions, is given below:

	Lot origin	
	Process A	Process B
Rule I . .	106	156
Rule II . .	55	177
Rule III . .	94	145
Rule IV . .	30	155

The selection of a particular rule under the appropriate choice criteria will be left to the reader.

Under some conditions, for the above kind of problem, monetary losses or gains cannot be assigned to the different eventualities. This situation will be considered in the next section.

EXERCISES—XIII

1. A lot of material is made available to a firm which is known to contain either 5 per cent or 10 per cent defective items. The quality control department is willing to use the lot 'as is' if it is 5 per cent defective. However, if it is 10 per cent defective a screening procedure is required. A screening procedure removes defective items. It is proposed to decide whether or not to screen the lot on the basis of inspecting a sample of size one. The alternative costs are as follows:

If the lot is screened and it is only 5 per cent defective, a loss of $3,000 is incurred.

If the lot is not screened and it is 10 per cent defective, a loss of $4,000 is incurred.

    (a) List four decision rules available to the firm.

    (b) Evaluate these rules and choose one using the minimax principle.

    (c) Assume that the probability that the lot is 5 per cent defective is known to be equal to 0·20. Which rule would be chosen?

2. Repeat the above if a sample of size ten is used.

3. The following decision rules are being considered by the manufacturer of an item which is made in lots of ten.

Rule A: (a) Take a random sample of one from a lot.

          (b) Test it and reject the lot if it is defective—otherwise accept the lot.

Rule B: (a) Take a random sample of size two from a lot.

          (b) Test the sample, if either item is defective, reject the lot—otherwise accept the lot. (Assume that both items are tested simultaneously.)

The monetary implications are as follows:

If a lot is accepted, then

(a) a profit of $200 is obtained for each good component and

(b) a loss of $75 is incurred for each defective component.

If a lot is rejected, then the manufacturer scraps the items and recovers for each item so disposed his production cost. The inspection is destructive and costs the firm $25 to perform for each item tested.

    (c) Evaluate each of these rules and choose one using the minimax principle.

    (d) Suppose that Rule B is modified so that items are not tested together and the lot is rejected without taking or testing the second item if the first is defective. Evaluate this modified rule.

4. A manufacturing process is such that it turns out 6,000 units per hour. The units are characterized by a particular dimension (X), known to be normally distributed with mean μ (unknown) and variance $\sigma^2 = 4$. Specifications call for items with dimensions between 19 and 11. The following decision rule is being considered:

        From the first hour's production, take four independent observations on the dimension of interest.

        If $\bar{X} \geqslant 17$ or if $\bar{X} \leqslant 13$, stop production and adjust the process.

Assume that it takes 20 minutes to adjust the process and that this time is lost from the next hour's production. Further, assume that the adjustment is such that once made it is known that μ will be and remain equal to 15 for the remaining production.

Find the expected number of good items produced during the second hour's production if the mean μ of the process when the observations were made was:

(a) 14.   (b) 15.   (c) 16.   (d) 17.

5. Repeat problem 4. Considering the same decision rule except that eight independent observations are to be made.

6. A buyer is faced with the problem of whether or not to accept a certain large lot of goods. It is a problem because the proportion of defectives, p, in the lot is unknown to him. If he accepts the lot, his profit will be $1,000 - 10,000p$ dollars. If he rejects the lot, he will lose 100 dollars.

Suppose he is considering using one of the following 2 decision rules:

Rule 1: Accept the lot without experimentation.
Rule 2: Select one item at random. If defective, reject the lot. Otherwise accept the lot.

(a) Compute the expected profit function for Rule 1.
(b) Compute the expected profit function for Rule 2.
(c) Which rule would you choose if you used a minimax choice principle?
(d) If p can be considered to be a random variable with density function

$$f_p: \quad f_p(a) = \begin{cases} 1 & \text{if } 0 \leqslant a \leqslant 1 \\ 0 & \text{otherwise} \end{cases}.$$

Compute the expected profit for Rule 1.
Compute the expected profit for Rule 2.
Which rule is preferable?

3.6. *Tests of hypotheses*

A special kind of decision problem arises frequently in scientific and engineering research. As in Example 3.10, it is of interest to decide to which of two classes of distribution functions the distribution function of a random variable, X, belongs. The problem is usually posed in the following form:

It is required to test the hypothesis that F_X belongs to a class of distribution functions, denoted by I, against the alternative hypothesis that it belongs to a different class denoted by II.

In Example 3.10, class I contained only one normal distribution function with parameters $\mu = 20$, $\sigma = 2$, while class II's only function (also normal) had parameters $\mu = 21$, $\sigma = 2$.

As another example, suppose that it is desirable to determine whether a coin is fair or not. Here we are interested in testing the hypothesis that $P(\text{heads}) = \frac{1}{2}$ against the alternative hypothesis that $P(\text{heads}) \neq \frac{1}{2}$. Class I consists only of the binomial distribution function with $p = \frac{1}{2}$, while class II contains all other binomial distribution functions with $p \neq \frac{1}{2}$.

As a rule, the hypothesis that F_X is in class I is called the '*null*' *hypothesis* (denoted by H_0). Usually, it represents some state of affairs descriptive of the *status quo* and containing no knowledge of a special or of an interesting nature. In the above case, the verification of the fairness of a coin would be an expected result, while the discovery that a coin was biased (the alternative hypothesis) would be an unusual phenomenon.

Our goal, as in other decision problems, is the selection of a good decision rule, which tells us which hypothesis to accept. Rules of this kind, because of the nature of the problem, are sometimes called 'tests'.

When a loss or gain structure is available, the techniques given in the preceding section are applicable. However, in many problems, especially those associated with exploratory research, it is not feasible to assess explicitly the value associated with alternative eventualities. Under these conditions, the conventional procedure is to introduce a function called the *operating characteristic* of the decision rule. This function specifies the loss structure in probabilistic terms.

Definition 3.4: The *operating characteristic* of a decision rule is the function, denoted by L, whose domain is the set of all distribution functions in class I and II and whose range is the probability of accepting the null hypothesis when using the given rule. That is,

$$L: \quad L(\theta) = \text{Probability of accepting the null}$$
$$\text{hypothesis } (H_0)$$

where θ denotes any distribution function of class I or II. The graph of the operating characteristic function is known as the *operating characteristic* (*OC*) *curve*.

In general, a favorable *OC* curve (i.e. a good decision rule) will take on values close to one for conditions under which the null hypothesis is true, and values close to zero for those situations associated with the alternative hypothesis being correct.

The approach in this section will be to consider, for several different problems, a class of decision rules having strong intuitive appeal. We shall indicate how the *OC* curve can be utilized to determine the required number of observations.

Problem I: A random variable X characterizes the output of a process. Suppose F_X is normal with mean μ (unknown) and standard deviation σ (known). Assume that the process is considered satisfactory when $\mu = \mu_0$, which is the usual circumstance. However, from time to time, it is considered desirable to check whether μ has 'slipped away' from μ_0. Assume no change can occur in σ.

Hence, we wish to test the null hypothesis

$$H_0: \quad \mu = \mu_0$$

against the alternative hypothesis

$$H_1: \quad \mu \neq \mu_0.$$

The class of decision rules considered for this problem is of the form:

(1) Take n independent observations on X.

(2) Reject H_0 if $|\bar{X} - \mu_0| > K$.

Note that K and n must be specified before the statement of the rule is complete.

A rule of the above form is usually called a 'two-sided rule'. This nomenclature has its origin in the location of the regions in which the null hypothesis will be rejected. In this case, these regions (sometimes called critical regions) are located on both sides of the region in which the null hypothesis would be accepted. In Problem II which follows, a one-sided rule is used.

The motivation for the choice of the above kind of decision rule is clear. Since $\bar{X}$ is a good estimator of μ, it will take on values close to μ_0 if μ_0 is the true value. If μ_0 is not the true value, then the greater the difference $|\mu - \mu_0|$, the more will $\bar{X}$ tend to deviate from μ_0. Hence, if $\bar{X}$ is far from μ_0, we are led to reject H_0.

The usual method of determining an appropriate value for K is to impose a condition on the operating characteristic function of the rule, motivated as follows:

If μ_0 is the true value of the parameter in question, i.e. if the null hypothesis is true, then we require that the probability of rejecting the null hypothesis be equal to some given value, denoted by α. Hence, we require that the OC function, i.e. the probability of accepting the null hypothesis, be equal to $1-\alpha$ when $\mu = \mu_0$.

Thus, *if H_0 is true*, the above condition states that

$$P\{\text{rejecting } H_0\} = P\{|\bar{X}-\mu_0| > K\} = \alpha$$

or

$$P\{\text{accepting } H_0\} = P\{|\bar{X}-\mu_0| \leqslant K\} = L(\mu_0) = (1-\alpha).$$

The stipulation of a value for α is equivalent to a partial specification of the loss or gain function in previously considered decision problems. Actually α will reflect the decision-maker's sense of the seriousness of the consequences involved in erroneously rejecting the null hypothesis. The number α is called the *level of significance*.

To find K, we note that under the null hypothesis, i.e. if $\mu = \mu_0$, the random variable $\bar{X}$ has a normal distribution with mean equal to μ_0 and variance equal to σ^2/n. Equivalently, the random variable $\dfrac{\bar{X}-\mu_0}{\sigma/\sqrt{n}}$ has a standard normal distribution.

Hence, in order that

$$P\{|\bar{X}-\mu_0| > K\} = P\left\{\frac{|\bar{X}-\mu_0|}{\sigma/\sqrt{n}} > \frac{K\sqrt{n}}{\sigma}\right\} = \alpha,$$

$(K\sqrt{n})/\sigma$ must be set equal to $K_{\frac{1}{2}\alpha}$ where $K_{\frac{1}{2}\alpha}$ is the value such that

$$\frac{1}{\sqrt{(2\pi)}} \int_{K_{\frac{1}{2}\alpha}}^{\infty} e^{-\frac{1}{2}t^2}\, dt = \tfrac{1}{2}\alpha$$

(i.e. the area to the right of $K_{\frac{1}{2}\alpha}$ under the standard normal density is $\tfrac{1}{2}\alpha$).

Thus, $$K = \frac{\sigma}{\sqrt{n}} K_{\frac{1}{2}\alpha}.$$

From the above it can be seen that part (2) of the decision rule may also be stated as

$$\text{Reject } H_0 \text{ if } \frac{|\overline{X} - \mu_0|}{\sigma/\sqrt{n}} > K_{\frac{1}{2}\alpha}.$$

This is usually the preferred form.

The operating characteristic function of the decision rule may be determined from the following considerations:

The null hypothesis will be accepted if the random variable $$\frac{|\overline{X} - \mu_0|}{\sigma/\sqrt{n}} \leqslant K_{\frac{1}{2}\alpha}.$$

Hence,

L: $L(\mu) = P$ {accepting H_0 when the true mean is μ}

$$= P\left\{\frac{|\overline{X} - \mu_0|}{\sigma/\sqrt{n}} \leqslant K_{\frac{1}{2}\alpha}\right\}$$

$$= P\left\{-K_{\frac{1}{2}\alpha} \leqslant \frac{\overline{X} - \mu_0}{\sigma/\sqrt{n}} \leqslant K_{\frac{1}{2}\alpha}\right\}$$

$$= P\left\{-K_{\frac{1}{2}\alpha} + \frac{\mu_0 - \mu}{\sigma/\sqrt{n}} \leqslant \left(\frac{\overline{X} - \mu}{\sigma/\sqrt{n}}\right) \leqslant K_{\frac{1}{2}\alpha} + \frac{\mu_0 - \mu}{\sigma/\sqrt{n}}\right\}.$$

However, the random variable $\left(\frac{\overline{X} - \mu}{\sigma/\sqrt{n}}\right)$ has a standard normal distribution. Consequently,

$$L: \quad L(\mu) = \frac{1}{\sqrt{(2\pi)}} \int\limits_{-K_{\frac{1}{2}\alpha} + \frac{\mu_0 - \mu}{\sigma/\sqrt{n}}}^{K_{\frac{1}{2}\alpha} + \frac{\mu_0 - \mu}{\sigma/\sqrt{n}}} e^{-\frac{1}{2}t^2}\, dt.$$

The OC curve corresponding to the above has an appearance similar to that shown in Figure 10.

In order to decide on the number n of observations to take, it is usual to impose another condition on the operating characteristic function. Suppose it is desired that the probability of accepting the null hypothesis be equal to some given risk, denoted by β, if $|\mu-\mu_0| = \delta$ (some pre-assigned value).

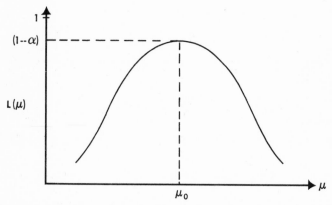

FIG. 10. *OC* curve for a decision rule of the type used in Problem I.

That is, it is required that

$$L(\mu_0+\delta) = \frac{1}{\sqrt{(2\pi)}} \int\limits_{-K_{\frac{1}{2}\alpha}-\frac{\delta}{\sigma/\sqrt{n}}}^{K_{\frac{1}{2}\alpha}-\frac{\delta}{\sigma/\sqrt{n}}} e^{-\frac{1}{2}t^2}\, dt = \beta.$$

NOTE: The stipulation of the value β completes the specification of the loss function for this decision problem. It should reflect the seriousness with which the decision maker regards accepting the null hypothesis when it is not true by an amount equal to δ.

Since n is the only unknown value, it may be found by appropriate manipulations. This may be accomplished approximately by assuming that the quantity

$$\left(-K_{\frac{1}{2}\alpha}-\frac{\delta}{\sigma/\sqrt{n}}\right)$$

is negative enough so that the area to the left of it, under the standard normal density function, may be considered negligible. Then, set

$$K_{\frac{1}{2}\alpha}-\frac{\delta}{\sigma/\sqrt{n}} = K_{1-\beta}$$

where $K_{1-\beta}$ is that value such that the probability that a standard normal random variable exceeds it is equal to $(1-\beta)$. Then we obtain

$$n \simeq \left[\frac{\sigma(K_{1-\beta}-K_{\frac{1}{2}\alpha})}{\delta}\right]^2.$$

Example 3.11: Suppose that in Problem I it is required to test

$$H_0: \quad u = 10$$

vs.

$$H_1: \quad u \neq 10$$

at level of significance $\alpha = 0 \cdot 10$, with the number of observations, n, such that if $\mu = 8$ or 12, then $\beta = 0 \cdot 20$. Assume $\sigma = 2$.

Since $\frac{1}{2}\alpha = 0 \cdot 05$, $K_{\frac{1}{2}\alpha} = 1 \cdot 64$, and $K_{1-\beta} = -0 \cdot 84$. Hence,

$$n \simeq \left[\frac{2(1 \cdot 64 + 0 \cdot 84)}{12 - 10}\right]^2 \simeq 7.$$

Suppose that the following observations have been made:

$$(10, \quad 9, \quad 10, \quad 11, \quad 13, \quad 12, \quad 12).$$

Thus, $\overline{X} = 11$. Using the rule indicated earlier, we would reject H_0 if

$$\frac{|\overline{X}-u_0|}{\sigma/\sqrt{n}} > K_{\frac{1}{2}\alpha}.$$

Consequently, we *accept* the null hypothesis, H_0, since

$$\frac{|11-10|}{2/\sqrt{7}} = 1 \cdot 32 \leqslant 1 \cdot 64.$$

On the other hand, suppose the following observations have been made:

$$(13, \quad 11, \quad 14, \quad 12, \quad 10, \quad 11, \quad 13).$$

Then, $\bar{X} = 12$. Using the rule, we would *reject* H_0 since

$$\frac{|12-10|}{2/\sqrt{7}} = \sqrt{7} > 1 \cdot 64.$$

Problem II: Two methods, denoted A and B, exist for tempering steel. Random variables X and Y represent the tensile strength (as determined by a standard test) of steel specimens produced by methods A and B respectively. It is of interest to decide whether process A yields specimens which have higher tensile strength than process B. Suppose, for example, that methods A and B are the same, except that A involves one additional, fairly expensive, operation.

Suppose it is assumed that random variables X and Y are each normally distributed with unknown means μ_A and μ_B and known variances σ_A^2 and σ_B^2. It is natural for this situation to formulate the null and alternative hypotheses as

$$H_0: \quad \mu_A = \mu_B,$$
$$H_1: \quad \mu_A > \mu_B.$$

The class of decision rules which we will consider for this problem is of the form:

(1) (a) Take n independent observations on X. This generates random variables $(X_1, ..., X_n)$.

    (b) Take m independent observations on Y. This generates random variables $(Y_1, ..., Y_m)$.

(2) Reject H_0 if $(\overline{X}-\overline{Y}) > K$ using a level of significance equal to α.

As mentioned earlier, this kind of rule is called a 'one-sided' rule. As in Problem I, it takes its name from the position of the region in which the null hypothesis is rejected. Such a region is used because we are only interested in rejecting H_0 when $\mu_A - \mu_B > 0$, a situation which is likely to be reflected by large values of $\overline{X}-\overline{Y}$.

To determine an appropriate value for K, we note that, from Theorem 7, the random variable

$$\left(\frac{(\overline{X}-\overline{Y})-(\mu_A-\mu_B)}{\sqrt{(\sigma_A^2/n+\sigma_B^2/m)}}\right)$$

has a standard normal distribution. Hence, if the null hypothesis is true, i.e. $\mu_A = \mu_B$, we may set

$$K = K_\alpha\sqrt{(\sigma_A^2/n+\sigma_B^2/m)}$$

where K_α is the value such that

$$P\left\{\left(\frac{(\overline{X}-\overline{Y})}{\sqrt{(\sigma_A^2/n+\sigma_B^2/m)}}\right) > K_\alpha\right\} = \frac{1}{\sqrt{(2\pi)}}\int_{K_\alpha}^{\infty} e^{-\frac{1}{2}t^2}\,dt = \alpha.$$

Letting $\Delta = (\mu_A-\mu_B)$, the operating characteristic function of the decision rule is given by

$$
\begin{aligned}
L:\quad L(\Delta) &= P\left\{\left(\frac{(\overline{X}-\overline{Y})}{\sqrt{(\sigma_A^2/n+\sigma_B^2/m)}}\right) \leqslant K_\alpha\right\} \\
&= P\left\{\left(\frac{(\overline{X}-\overline{Y})-\Delta}{\sqrt{(\sigma_A^2/n+\sigma_B^2/m)}}\right) \leqslant K_\alpha - \frac{\Delta}{\sqrt{(\sigma_A^2/n+\sigma_B^2/m)}}\right\} \\
&= \frac{1}{\sqrt{(2\pi)}}\int_{-\infty}^{K_\alpha-\frac{\Delta}{\sqrt{(\sigma_A^2/n+\sigma_B^2/m)}}} e^{-\frac{1}{2}t^2}\,dt.
\end{aligned}
$$

The number of observations n and m may now be determined. First, we note that for any value of $\Delta > 0$, it is obviously desirable that $L(\Delta)$ be as small as possible. This is accomplished by having

$$\frac{\Delta}{\sqrt{(\sigma_A^2/n + \sigma_B^2/m)}}$$

in the above expression, as large as possible. This, in turn, implies that $G = \sigma_A^2/n + \sigma_B^2/m$ should be at a minimum. The relationship between m and n is obtained by differentiating G with respect to m or n, setting the derivative equal to zero and solving. This yields

$$\frac{m}{n} = \frac{\sigma_B}{\sigma_A}.$$

Let $N = m + n$, then it can be shown that

$$\frac{\sigma_A^2}{n} + \frac{\sigma_B^2}{m} = \frac{(\sigma_A + \sigma_B)^2}{N}.$$

Suppose that it is stipulated that if $\Delta = \Delta_0 > 0$, then $L(\Delta_0) = \beta$. N is now chosen so that

$$K_\alpha - \frac{\Delta_0}{\sqrt{(\sigma_A^2/n + \sigma_B^2/m)}} = K_\alpha - \frac{\Delta_0}{\sqrt{\{(\sigma_A + \sigma_B)^2/N\}}} = K_{1-\beta}$$

where $K_{1-\beta}$ is the number such that the probability that a standard normal random variable exceeds it is equal to $(1-\beta)$. Thus,

$$N = \frac{(K_{1-\beta} - K_\alpha)^2 (\sigma_A + \sigma_B)^2}{\Delta_0^2}.$$

Since $m/n = \sigma_B/\sigma_A$ and $m + n = N$, it follows that

$$n = \frac{N}{(\sigma_B/\sigma_A) + 1}.$$

Problem III: Suppose that X has a normal distribution with parameters μ and σ, both unknown. It is required to test, at α level of significance,

$$H_0: \quad \mu = \mu_0,$$
vs.
$$H_1: \quad \mu \neq \mu_0.$$

An appropriate decision rule is of the class:

(1) Take n independent observations on X, generating the random variables $(X_1, ..., X_n)$.

(2) Reject H_0 if the random variable

$$\left(\frac{|\overline{X} - \mu_0|}{s/\sqrt{n}} \right) > t_{\frac{1}{2}\alpha}$$

where

$$s = \sqrt{\left(\frac{1}{n-1} \sum_{i=1}^{n} (X_i - \overline{X})^2 \right)}.$$

Note that since σ is unknown, it is reasonable to use a rule similar to that of Problem I with σ replaced by s.

It can be shown that the random variable $\left(\dfrac{\overline{X} - \mu_0}{s/\sqrt{n}} \right)$ has a Student's t-distribution with parameter $\nu = (n-1)$ degrees of freedom (see Table V). Hence, $t_{\frac{1}{2}\alpha}$ may be found as that value such that the probability that a random variable, having a Student's t-distribution with $(n-1)$ degrees of freedom, exceeds it is equal to $\frac{1}{2}\alpha$.

The above is sometimes referred to as a 'two-sided t-test'.

The operating characteristic function is given by

$$L(\mu) = P\{\text{accepting } H_0\}$$
$$= P\left\{ -t_{\frac{1}{2}\alpha} < \left(\frac{\overline{X} - \mu_0}{s/\sqrt{n}} \right) < t_{\frac{1}{2}\alpha} \right\},$$

where the random variable $\left(\dfrac{\overline{X}-\mu_0}{s/\sqrt{n}}\right)$ has a 'non-central t-distribution'.† This distribution has two parameters. One is called the degrees of freedom, which for this case is equal to $(n-1)$. The other parameter may be denoted by δ where $\delta = \left(\dfrac{\sqrt{n}(\mu-\mu_0)}{\sigma}\right)$. It is usually convenient to express the OC function using $\delta/\sqrt{n}$ as the value in the domain.

Given the set of OC functions for all possible values of n, one may select an appropriate sample size in the same fashion as in Problem I.

Problem IV: Suppose that a purchasing agent is offered a lot containing N items. He has the privilege of either purchasing or refusing the lot in its entirety. Assume that if the proportion of defectives in the lot (p) is less than some given value (p_0), he would be willing to accept the lot.

A possible decision rule is

(1) Select an item from the lot at random, inspect it, classify it as defective or non-defective, and then return it to the lot. Repeat, until n observations have been made. This is known as 'sampling with replacement.'

(2) Reject the lot if the number of defectives, denoted by the random variable Y, exceeds some fixed number K. That is, reject the lot if $Y > K$.

Such a rule is called a *single sampling plan*.

† An extensive tabulation of this distribution is given in Resnikoff, G. J., and Lieberman, G. J., *Tables of the Non-central t-Distribution*, Stanford University Press and Oxford University Press, 1957. See in particular p. 23.

Since Y has a binomial distribution with parameter p, the OC function is given by

$$L: \quad L(p) = P\{Y \leqslant K\}$$
$$= \sum_{s=0}^{K} \binom{n}{s} p^s (1-p)^{n-s}.$$

If, as before, $L(p_0)$ is set to equal $(1-\alpha)$ and if for some $p_1 > p_0$ the value $L(p_1)$ is set equal to β, where α and β are pertinent preassigned risk values, it is possible to determine both n and K.

For computational convenience, the above probability function is usually approximated using either the normal or Poisson distribution. Practically, however, this is not necessary, since extensive catalogues of such plans and the associated OC functions exist.†

3.7. *Confidence interval estimation*

As discussed earlier, in problems of testing hypotheses, there are occasions when the ultimate decisions and their consequent losses are somewhat removed from the immediate problem. Similarly, all that is required for some other situations is an estimate of a property of a distribution function together with some notion of the precision associated with the experiment used to obtain this estimate.

For example, if an investigator measures a physical constant, he usually describes his result in the form of a number which represents his most informed guess of the true value of the constant, together with an estimate of the precision of his measurement technique. The precision

† For example, see Mil-Std-105 A, *Sampling Procedures and Tables for Inspection by Attributes*, U.S. Government Printing Office, Washington 25, D.C.

is commonly indicated in the form of an interval on either side of the estimated true value.

Thus, it is desirable to be able to specify an interval which may reasonably be expected to include the true value of a property of a distribution function.

Let θ denote the property in question. The confidence interval approach to estimation consists in defining a rule of the following kind:

(1) Take a sample of n independent observations on X. Denote these by $(X_1,...,X_n)$.

(2) Form two functions (random variables)

$$G_1: \quad G_1(X_1,...,X_n)$$

and $\quad\quad G_2: \quad G_2(X_1,...,X_n),$

where $G_1 < G_2$, such that

$$P\{G_1(X_1,...,X_n) < \theta < G_2(X_1,...,X_n)\} = (1-\alpha)$$

and where $(1-\alpha)$ is some preassigned value.

In other words, G_1 and G_2 form a random interval which will vary from sample to sample and which may or may not, in any given case, contain the true value of θ. However, the frequency interpretation of the above probability statement is that, on the average, an interval so chosen by the rule will contain the true value θ a proportion of times equal to the given value $(1-\alpha)$. It is obviously desirable to have the length of the interval, G_2-G_1, as small as possible, consistent with the above preassigned probability.

It is usual to speak of a $100(1-\alpha)$ *per cent confidence interval*, where $(1-\alpha)$ is defined as above.

Three important examples will illustrate this approach.

Problem V: Assume that X has a normal distribution with parameters μ (unknown) and σ^2 (known). A confidence interval estimate of μ is required.

It will be recalled that the random variable $\left(\dfrac{\overline{X}-\mu}{\sigma/\sqrt{n}}\right)$ has a standard normal distribution. Hence, we may choose a number $C_{\frac{1}{2}\alpha}$ such that

$$(1-\alpha) = P\left\{-C_{\frac{1}{2}\alpha} < \left(\frac{\overline{X}-\mu}{\sigma/\sqrt{n}}\right) < C_{\frac{1}{2}\alpha}\right\} = \frac{1}{\sqrt{(2\pi)}} \int_{-C_{\frac{1}{2}\alpha}}^{C_{\frac{1}{2}\alpha}} e^{-\frac{1}{2}t^2} dt.$$

Multiplying by $\sigma/\sqrt{n}$ and subtracting $\overline{X}$ from each of the terms, yields

$$(1-\alpha) = P\{\overline{X}-C_{\frac{1}{2}\alpha}\sigma/\sqrt{n} < \mu < \overline{X}+C_{\frac{1}{2}\alpha}\sigma/\sqrt{n}\}.$$

Hence, the required functions are

$$G_1: \quad G_1(X_1,...,X_n) = \overline{X}-C_{\frac{1}{2}\alpha}\sigma/\sqrt{n}$$

and $\quad G_2: \quad G_2(X_1,...,X_n) = \overline{X}+C_{\frac{1}{2}\alpha}\sigma/\sqrt{n}.$

Notice that the length of the interval is

$$(G_2-G_1) = 2C_{\frac{1}{2}\alpha}\sigma/\sqrt{n}.$$

Thus, if it is desired to have a confidence interval of some prescribed length δ, i.e. to have a preassigned precision along with the preassigned probability $(1-\alpha)$, we can set $\quad (G_2-G_1) = \delta$

and solve for n, the required number of observations. This yields

$$n = \frac{4C_{\frac{1}{2}\alpha}^2\sigma^2}{\delta^2}.$$

Problem VI: Suppose that X has a normal distribution with parameters μ and σ^2, both unknown.

If
$$s^2 = \frac{1}{n-1} \sum_{i=1}^{n} (X_i - \bar{X})^2$$

then it can be shown that the random variable $\left(\dfrac{\bar{X}-\mu}{s/\sqrt{n}}\right)$ has a Student's t-distribution with parameter $(n-1)$ degrees of freedom. Consequently, using the same method as in Problem V, except that $C_{\frac12 \alpha}$ is obtained from tables of the Student's t-distribution, the required functions are

$$G_1: \quad G_1(X_1,...,X_n) = \bar{X} - C_{\frac12 \alpha} s/\sqrt{n},$$
$$G_2: \quad G_2(X_1,...,X_n) = \bar{X} + C_{\frac12 \alpha} s/\sqrt{n}.$$

It may be noted that the length of the confidence interval is $2C_{\frac12 \alpha} s/\sqrt{n}$, i.e. the length will depend upon the observations $(X_1,...,X_n)$ as reflected in the computed value of s. Thus, it is not possible, in this case, to predetermine the interval length by taking a fixed number of observations.

Problem VII: Assume that X has a normal distribution and that a $100(1-\alpha)$ per cent confidence interval estimate is required of the variance σ^2.

It can be shown that the random variable $[(n-1)s^2/\sigma^2]$ has a chi-square distribution with parameter equal to $(n-1)$ degrees of freedom.

Thus, by choosing the values $C_{1-\frac12 \alpha}$ and $C_{\frac12 \alpha}$ from tables of the chi-square distribution,† we have

$$(1-\alpha) = P\left\{ C_{1-\frac12 \alpha} < \left(\frac{(n-1)s^2}{\sigma^2}\right) < C_{\frac12 \alpha}\right\}$$
$$= P\left\{\frac{(n-1)s^2}{C_{\frac12 \alpha}} < \sigma^2 < \frac{(n-1)s^2}{C_{1-\frac12 \alpha}}\right\}.$$

† See Table VI.

Therefore, the required functions are

$$G_1: \quad G_1(X_1,...,X_n) = \frac{(n-1)s^2}{C_{\frac{1}{2}\alpha}},$$

$$G_2: \quad G_2(X_1,...,X_n) = \frac{(n-1)s^2}{C_{1-\frac{1}{2}\alpha}}.$$

EXERCISES—XIV

1. It is known that a particular machine produces nails whose length is a random variable having a normal distribution with constant variance equal to 0·0001.

Experiments have been conducted yielding the following results:
$$1·14, \ 1·15, \ 1·14, \ 1·12, \ 1·13.$$

   (a) Test the hypothesis that $\mu = 1·12$. Use the alternative hypothesis that $\mu \neq 1·12$ and a 0·01 level of significance.
   (b) Sketch the *OC* curve for the above rule.

2. It is desired to test at a 0·02 level of significance the hypothesis

$$H_0: \quad \mu = 20$$
$$\text{vs.} \quad H_1: \quad \mu > 20$$

so that the probability of accepting the null hypothesis is equal to 0·10 if $\mu = 0·22$.

   (a) Assuming that $\sigma = 2$, determine the number of observations to take.
   (b) Determine the number of observations to take if the test is to be performed at a 0·10 level of significance.

3. $X_1,..., X_4$ are independent normal random variables with common mean μ (unknown) and common variance equal to 4.

   It is desired to test
$$H_0: \quad \mu = 18$$
$$\text{vs.} \quad H_1: \quad \mu > 18$$

using the decision rule: Reject H_0 if $(\overline{X} - 18) > 1$.

   If H_0 is rejected when true, a loss equal to 1,000 occurs.

   If H_0 is accepted when it is false, a loss of 500 is involved.

   If H_0 is either accepted when true or rejected when false, no losses are incurred.

(a) Compute the probability of rejecting the null hypothesis when it is true when using the above decision rule.

(b) Compute the expected loss if $\mu = 16, 17, 18, 19$.

4. Let $X_1,\ldots, X_9$ be 9 independently and normally distributed random variables each of which have a common mean μ (unknown) and variance 2. It is of interest to test the hypothesis that $\mu = 10$ against the alternative that $\mu \neq 10$.

A loss $3|\mu - 10|$ is sustained if the hypothesis $\mu = 10$ is accepted when in fact $\mu \neq 10$. If $\mu = 10$ then a loss of 20 is sustained if the hypothesis that $\mu = 10$ is rejected.

A proposed decision rule is:

Reject the hypothesis if $|\bar{X} - 10| > 2$ and accept it otherwise.

Compute the expected loss if $\mu = 8, 9, 10, 11, 12$.

5. It has been suggested that the resistance of wire A is greater than the resistance of wire B. Tests made on samples of each wire yielded the following results:

A	B
0·140 ohms	0·135 ohms
0·138	0·140
0·143	0·142
0·142	0·136
0·144	0·138
0·137	

(a) Assuming normality and that $\sigma_A = 0.002$, $\sigma_B = 0.003$, settle the argument.

(b) Sketch the OC curve for the decision rule used in (a).

6. It is known that the number of automobile accidents on summer week-ends has a Poisson distribution with parameter $\lambda = 100$.

A vigorous safety campaign of a certain type was conducted for a period of time. At the end of this period, the observed number of accidents on three week-ends was found to be equal to 85, 75, 80. Would you infer from the above that the safety campaign has been effective? (NOTE: See problem 8, Exercises X.)

7. Derive a single sampling plan (for sampling with replacement) such that the probability of accepting lots which contain 5 per cent defective material is 0·90 and the probability of rejecting lots which contain 10 per cent defective material is 0·90.

8. A standard drug is known to be effective in 80 per cent of cases in which it is used to treat infections. A new drug has been found effective in 85 of the first 100 cases tried. Is the superiority of the new drug well established?

9. An optimal ordering policy for inventory of lumber in board-feet has been developed for a lumber company. The policy assumes that daily demand for inventory in board-feet is an independently distributed normal random variable with mean equal to 40,000 board-feet and unknown variance. The firm wishes to test this assumption, using the records of daily demand for the past week (five days). If the assumption is not valid, the company wishes to change the ordering policy. The firm is willing to risk, with probability equal to 0·01, changing the ordering policy if

$$\mu = 40,000.$$

  (a) State a decision rule for accomplishing the above result.
  (b) Given the following record of daily demand for the past week, should the ordering policy be revised?

    40,111; 42,350; 37,250; 39,338; 41,751.

10. It is known that a particular machine produces nails whose length is a random variable having a normal distribution with an expected value directly related to the machine setting and with a constant variance equal to 0·0001.

  Experiments have been conducted at several different machine settings yielding the following results:

Setting 1	Setting 2	Setting 3
1·14 inches	1·46 inches	1·77 inches
1·15	1·52	1·75
1·14	1·52	1·76
1·12	1·53	1·75
1·13	1·50	1·77

  (a) Compute 99 per cent confidence limits for μ related to each setting.
  (b) Compute 90 per cent confidence limits for μ related to each setting.
  (c) How many observations would have to be made so that there would be a probability equal to 0·80 of including the expected value in a confidence interval of length equal to 0·1? of length equal to 0·01?

TABLE IV. *Selected values of the standard normal cumulative distribution function*

$$\Phi: \quad \Phi(a) = \frac{1}{\sqrt{(2\pi)}} \int_{-\infty}^{a} e^{-\frac{1}{2}t^2} \, dt$$

a	$\Phi(a)$	a	$\Phi(a)$
$-3 \cdot 0$	0·001	0·1	0·540
$-2 \cdot 9$	0·002	0·2	0·579
$-2 \cdot 8$	0·003	0·3	0·618
$-2 \cdot 7$	0·004	0·4	0·655
$-2 \cdot 6$	0·005	0·5	0·691
$-2 \cdot 5$	0·006	0·6	0·726
$-2 \cdot 4$	0·008	0·7	0·758
$-2 \cdot 33$	0·010	0·8	0·788
$-2 \cdot 3$	0·011	0·9	0·816
$-2 \cdot 2$	0·014	1·0	0·841
$-2 \cdot 1$	0·018	1·1	0·864
$-2 \cdot 0$	0·023	1·2	0·885
$-1 \cdot 96$	0·025	1·28	0·900
$-1 \cdot 9$	0·029	1·3	0·903
$-1 \cdot 8$	0·036	1·4	0·919
$-1 \cdot 7$	0·045	1·5	0·933
$-1 \cdot 64$	0·050	1·6	0·945
$-1 \cdot 6$	0·055	1·64	0·950
$-1 \cdot 5$	0·067	1·7	0·955
$-1 \cdot 4$	0·081	1·8	0·964
$-1 \cdot 3$	0·097	1·9	0·971
$-1 \cdot 28$	0·100	1·96	0·975
$-1 \cdot 2$	0·115	2·0	0·977
$-1 \cdot 1$	0·136	2·1	0·982
$-1 \cdot 0$	0·159	2·2	0·986
$-0 \cdot 9$	0·184	2·3	0·989
$-0 \cdot 8$	0·212	2·33	0·990
$-0 \cdot 7$	0·242	2·4	0·992
$-0 \cdot 6$	0·274	2·5	0·994
$-0 \cdot 5$	0·309	2·6	0·995
$-0 \cdot 4$	0·345	2·7	0·996
$-0 \cdot 3$	0·382	2·8	0·997
$-0 \cdot 2$	0·421	2·9	0·998
$-0 \cdot 1$	0·460	3·0	0·999
0	0·500		

TABLE V. *Selected values of the cumulative Student's t-distribution function*†

$$F: \quad F(a) = \int_{-\infty}^{a} \frac{\{\tfrac{1}{2}(\nu-1)\}!(1+t^2/\nu)^{-\tfrac{1}{2}(\nu+1)}}{\{\tfrac{1}{2}(\nu-2)\}!\sqrt{(\pi\nu)}} \, dt$$

Degrees of freedom ν	$F(a)$				
	0·90	0·95	0·975	0·99	0·995
1	3·08	6·31	12·7	31·8	63·7
2	1·89	2·92	4·30	6·96	9·92
3	1·64	2·35	3·18	4·54	5·84
4	1·53	2·13	2·78	3·75	4·60
5	1·48	2·02	2·57	3·36	4·03
6	1·44	1·94	2·45	3·14	3·71
7	1·41	1·90	2·36	3·00	3·50
8	1·40	1·86	2·31	2·90	3·36
9	1·38	1·83	2·26	2·82	3·25
10	1·37	1·81	2·23	2·76	3·17
11	1·36	1·80	2·20	2·72	3·11
12	1·36	1·78	2·18	2·68	3·06
13	1·35	1·77	2·16	2·65	3·01
14	1·34	1·76	2·14	2·62	2·98
15	1·34	1·75	2·13	2·60	2·95
16	1·34	1·75	2·12	2·58	2·92
17	1·33	1·74	2·11	2·57	2·90
18	1·33	1·73	2·10	2·55	2·88
19	1·33	1·73	2·09	2·54	2·86
20	1·32	1·72	2·09	2·53	2·84
21	1·32	1·72	2·08	2·52	2·83
22	1·32	1·72	2·07	2·51	2·82
23	1·32	1·71	2·07	2·50	2·81
24	1·32	1·71	2·06	2·49	2·80
25	1·32	1·71	2·06	2·48	2·79
26	1·31	1·71	2·06	2·48	2·78
27	1·31	1·70	2·05	2·47	2·77
28	1·31	1·70	2·05	2·47	2·76
29	1·31	1·70	2·05	2·46	2·76
30	1·31	1·70	2·04	2·46	2·75
40	1·30	1·68	2·02	2·42	2·70
60	1·30	1·67	2·00	2·39	2·66
120	1·29	1·66	1·98	2·36	2·62
∞	1·28	1·64	1·96	2·33	2·58

† This table is abridged from Table III of Fisher and Yates, *Statistical Tables for Biological, Agricultural, and Medical Research*, published by Oliver and Boyd Ltd., Edinburgh. By permission of the authors and the publishers.

TABLE VI. *Selected values of the χ^2 cumulative distribution function*†

$$F: \quad F(a) = \int_0^a \frac{t^{\frac{1}{2}(\nu-2)}e^{-\frac{1}{2}t}}{2^{\nu/2}\{\frac{1}{2}(\nu-2)\}!} \, dt$$

Degrees of freedom ν	$F(a)$							
	0·01	0·025	0·05	0·10	0·90	0·95	0·975	0·99
1	0·000157	0·000982	0·00393	0·0158	2·71	3·84	5·02	6·63
2	0·0201	0·0506	0·103	0·211	4·61	5·99	7·38	9·21
3	0·115	0·216	0·352	0·584	6·25	7·81	9·35	11·3
4	0·297	0·484	0·711	1·06	7·78	9·49	11·1	13·3
5	0·554	0·831	1·15	1·61	9·24	11·1	12·8	15·1
6	0·872	1·24	1·64	2·20	10·6	12·6	14·4	16·8
7	1·24	1·69	2·17	2·83	12·0	14·1	16·0	18·5
8	1·65	2·18	2·73	3·49	13·4	15·5	17·5	20·1
9	2·09	2·70	3·33	4·17	14·7	16·9	19·0	21·7
10	2·56	3·25	3·94	4·87	16·0	18·3	20·5	23·2
11	3·05	3·82	4·57	5·58	17·3	19·7	21·9	24·7
12	3·57	4·40	5·23	6·30	18·5	21·0	23·3	26·2
13	4·11	5·01	5·89	7·04	19·8	22·4	24·7	27·7
14	4·66	5·63	6·57	7·79	21·1	23·7	26·1	29·1
15	5·23	6·26	7·26	8·55	22·3	25·0	27·5	30·6
16	5·81	6·91	7·96	9·31	23·5	26·3	28·8	32·0
17	6·41	7·56	8·67	10·1	24·8	27·6	30·2	33·4
18	7·01	8·23	9·39	10·9	26·0	28·9	31·5	34·8
19	7·63	8·91	10·1	11·7	27·2	30·1	32·9	36·2
20	8·26	9·59	10·9	12·4	28·4	31·4	34·2	37·6
25	11·5	13·1	14·6	16·5	34·4	37·7	40·6	44·3
30	15·0	16·8	18·5	20·6	40·3	43·8	47·0	50·9
35	18·5	20·6	22·5	24·8	46·1	49·8	53·2	57·3
40	22·2	24·4	26·5	29·1	51·8	55·8	59·3	63·7
45	25·9	28·4	30·6	33·4	57·5	61·7	65·4	70·0
50	29·7	32·4	34·8	37·7	63·2	67·5	71·4	76·2
60	37·5	40·5	43·2	46·5	74·4	79·1	83·3	88·4
70	45·4	48·8	51·7	55·3	85·5	90·5	95·0	100·4
80	53·5	57·2	60·4	64·3	96·6	101·9	106·6	112·3
90	61·8	65·6	69·1	73·3	107·6	113·1	118·1	124·1
100	70·1	74·2	77·9	82·4	118·5	124·3	129·6	135·8

† This table has been abridged from A. Hald and S. A. Sinkbaek, *A Table of Percentage Points of the χ^2 Distribution*, Skandinavisk Aktuarietidskrift, 1950. By permission of the authors.